THE SPIRIT OF THE SCORPION
Second Edition

Conquering the Powers of Insurrection

by John L. Mastrogiovanni, D.Min.

Copyright © 1992, 2010

Bold lettering is used by the author to emphasize segments within scriptures quoted.

TABLE OF CONTENTS

PROLOGUE

Time and time again we find churches splitting, disunity in the congregation, people wounded, and the innocent being sacrificed on the altars of manipulation and control. How many times have churches found the supposed *spiritual believer* causing invaluable members to be disloyal and stray from their pastoral leaders? In recent years there have been too many occasions of self-appointed prophets, intercessors and ministers who prowled into churches, poisoning innocent lambs with toxic partial truths regarding leadership and spiritual vision. This all results in altered steadfastness and brings about naive mutiny against the mission of the local church.

Few men and women respond to the call of God with the desire to have their ministry split or the intent to make a mistake that would plague the ministry with frustration and revolt. Yet it seems the powers of darkness would cause many to believe otherwise and are ever trying to discredit men and women in the hearts of the faithful.

Unfortunately, we realize the specific wiles of the enemy either during or after the apex of the situation. The point of this book is to bring our awareness, as church leaders and congregational members, to the engagement and stratagem of this particular adversary who incites *insurrection* and *cessation*. Although this book is basically written to church leaders, those who are working with and submitted to them can also benefit from its information. For some, the following pages will open their eyes. For others, they will simply realize what they have always known in their hearts.

 **CHAPTER 1**

SCORPION PASS

Of all the challenges men and women of God face in ministry life, there seems to be none more devastating than betrayal. All the ministerial training and mentoring, the years of experience and theological knowledge, cannot prepare us for that moment. Yet it happens more often than we would like to think. Even more so, it happens in the most subtle ways so that when the church leader realizes insurrection has taken place, *he may even blame himself.*

When the subtle workings of insurrection have been successful, blaming yourself for poor leadership, bad organizational abilities, lack of spirituality, or even just plain blindness, never appears to be the solution or points to the real reason. Nonetheless, such feelings tend to overwhelm your every thought. In many cases the choice to be more diplomatic is made, or to attend more leadership training seminars, or to compensate by seeking validation from the wrong people, rather than administering strong but loving correction.

Think about insurrection. Was it caused

because of poor leadership or inabilities that allowed a person to grow close to you, to share your heart, only to use your simple human weaknesses as a tool to lead others in another direction? Was it your lack of spirituality that gave the privilege of authority over an area of ministry to a person that seemed to partake of your vision and love for the ministry? The answer is a simple, *"No."* We need to see insurrection for what it is and call it what it is. Judas was not on a heavenly mission to lead God's people in a better direction. Korah was not called to save the people from Moses' lack of spirituality. *The fact is, there was a carnal attitude and a spiritual force at work to hinder what God intended, as well as God's leader.*

I have watched many friends in ministry over the years go through a lot of unnecessary pain with staff members, elders and fellow laborers. In some cases, it wounded them for years. I call this *unnecessary pain* because the issues these leaders went through and were accused of were hardly anything of significance. In some occasions, the accusations weren't even close to the truth. They weren't living in perpetual sin, they didn't abuse ministry funds, and they were not behaving inappropriately with the opposite sex. They were just targets of darkness to cripple the work of God and stain the image of Christ in them.

Several years ago, I sat at lunch with a wonderful pastor who truly lives a holy life. He told me of an elder in his church who felt it was his mission to send "anonymous" letters to all the leadership. The elder believed that the teachings of the pastor were heretical, but would not confront him to his face. Finally, when asked about it directly by the pastor at an elders' meeting, the individual lied, not wanting to be exposed. When the pastor began to apply pressure on him with proof, he finally admitted what he did. This kind of trauma should not plague local church pastors and elders. But these things happen to many men and women of God. In most cases, it is tolerated because of manipulation or fear of the rippling affect on the congregation, but it is in no way the design of God.

After pastoring for many years and facing such challenges more than once myself, I have come to call such situations *Scorpion Pass.* I began to realize the gravity of this spiritual pass when a church in our city went through six pastors in about ten years. That's when I began to pray and ask God what was happening from a larger scope. It was then I found the comfort of the scripture:

> *"Behold, I give you the authority to trample on serpents and scorpions, and over all the power of the enemy, and nothing shall by any means hurt you." (Luke 10:19/NKJV)*

But then a question arose in my heart. I have heard many messages on the serpent and its wiles, but what of this thing called **the Scorpion?** Jesus said we would tread on this creature. I knew He would not have used it as an example unless there was some spiritual parallel.

This is what I found:

"Your southern side will include some of the Desert of Zin along the border of Edom. On the east, your southern boundary will start from the end of the Salt Sea, cross south of **Scorpion Pass,** *continue on to Zin and go south of Kadesh Barnea."*

(Numbers 34:3-4/NIV)

In the above verses, God was describing to the children of Israel where the borders of their inheritance were in the land of Canaan. In the southern part of the land, there was a place called Scorpion Pass. It was a very dry and elevated desert area. Because it was elevated, it was exposed to constant heat with little possibility of shade. This place was a scorpion's haven. These arachnids relish living in dry territories and covertly blend into the landscape. Because of this, they also sleep during the day and prowl around in the darkness of the night.

If you were to walk through this waterless haven, there is a strong chance you would encounter one. If you were to camp there throughout the night, you would be in real danger of a painful and possibly deadly encounter. Most of the time, individuals stumble upon such a route unawares. By the time a person realizes that they have confronted a scorpion, they have already been impaled by it. The scorpion, however, sensed his prey approaching for quite a while!

Scorpions have intuitive, sensor-like hairs on their body and a keen sense of smell. In other words, a scorpion can detect its food coming long before it delivers its stinging presence. Furthermore, the scorpion is exclusively carnivorous. In other words, they are flesh eaters. They can go without food for long periods of time, so they don't mind waiting and being selective. If a creature is in close proximity, the scorpion lunges forth without warning, grabs its prey with its front claws, swings its poisonous tail *(unseen by the victim)* over its head and stings it. In just a few seconds the victim is paralyzed by the venom[MA3].

Since a scorpion does not have conventional jaws, it holds its food in its mouth with a pair of tooth-like appendages and vomits[MA4] up digestive fluids from the small intestine. The victim's soft parts are then liquefied and sucked into the stomach by a pumping action. While serpents strike and eat their victims whole, the scorpion meticulously takes its victim apart piece by piece. This is why many times it's not until the apex, the height of the situation, that we realize something has been eroding the unity of the congregation.

A scorpion's mating habits are not any lovelier than its eating habits. After a drawn-out mating dance, moving sideways, forward and backwards, the moment arrives for copulation. When the deed is done[MA5], there is a black widow-like turn of events: if the male remains anywhere near the female, she devours him as an after-romance snack.

Scorpion Pass is not a place I would want to travel through for any reason, much less camp in! **But many believers and leaders have found this**

kind of scenario in their own churches. So how does an individual molt into a scorpion? The answer is found in the condition of the believer's heart. If their heart is a desert (a dry place), this can only mean that they left the moisture of the rivers of Living Water. Cool, well-watered gardens are not breeding grounds for scorpions, nor do they turn into deserts. If we are firmly planted in the vibrancy of God's spiritual character, we will never dry out.

> *"He is like a tree planted by streams of water, which yields its fruit in season and whose leaf does not wither. Whatever he does prospers." (Psalms 1:3/NKJV)*

> *"Whoever believes in me, as the Scripture has said, streams of living water will flow from within him.' By this he meant the Spirit, whom those who believed in him were later to receive..." (John 7:38-39/NKJV)*

When an individual leaves the "main stream" of what the Holy Spirit is doing in his local church or ministry, it is inevitable that he will dry out. Whenever a person becomes part of the fringe and not a true vision holder with the leadership and congregation, he will develop the dryness of *self-gratification*. In some cases, self-gratification molts into self-exaltation and he becomes elevated with pride, a perfect breeding ground for the spirit of the Scorpion.

> *"O foolish Galatians! Who has bewitched you that you should not obey the truth, before whose eyes Jesus Christ was clearly portrayed*

among you as crucified? This only I want to learn from you: Did you receive the Spirit by the works of the law, or by the hearing of faith? Are you so foolish? Having begun in the Spirit, are you now being made perfect by the flesh?" (Galatians 3:1-3/NKJV)

When a person begins to "dry out" and he doesn't return to the place where he stepped out of the flow of *God's Corporate Spirit,* he is in big trouble. Leaving those rivers of Living Water and trying to mature through some other means (works of the flesh) breeds arrogance. Keep in mind that when a person becomes a desert, he opens himself up to a lot of dangerous, venomous creatures like vipers and scorpions. The problem lies in the fact that he has fooled himself into believing that if he walks in the manifestations of the Spirit (listed in 1 Corinthians 12) and reads his Bible every day, he won't dry out. But that is not spiritual reality! According to Romans 11:29 and Matthew 7:22-23, one can manifest gifts of the Holy Spirit whether living rightly or not, hence anyone can still be a desert. According to Luke 13:26-27 and John 5:39, knowledge of scripture will not save or preserve you in Christ, either. Consequently, our misplaced confidence can produce a Scorpion Pass. *The only saving and preserving reality is a faith that produces heart-yielding fruit.*

A healthy person is a person who has learned to be a functional, fruitful part of the congregation. When a person is fruitful in his spiritual life, he will always seek to give life to the congregation. Yet as one becomes a desert, and scorpion-like attitudes form, he will seek the innocent flesh of others to thrive and reproduce. Rather than giving life to the congregation, the congregation becomes his prey.

It is usually the unsuspecting believer who becomes the scorpion's victim. Most of the time, **when a victim has been grabbed, he will be paralyzed by the sting of the subtle, bitter information he is given.** The whole point is to divert the loyalty of that church member to the one who has the "special information." Once the scorpion[MA6] has the victim in his grip, he will begin to vomit all the lies, arrogance, self-importance and bitterness he has developed. In the end (if the victimized person doesn't break free) he will either be consumed with fear, leaving the church possibly never to return, or will mate with the scorpion which will produce others. The only true defense to the wiles of the scorpion is *the Character of God.* Keep in mind, this does not mean simply having an understanding of what God's character is, but living a life that *demonstrates* His character.

In the early church, before the New Testament was ever canonized, every believer still had to live a life that demonstrated God's character. In other words, they had to bear the fruit of the Spirit. Even the church at Corinth, which functioned in the manifestations and expressions of the Holy Spirit, was exhorted to go on with God by a more excellent way: *The way of love,* the fruit of the Spirit (1 Corinthians 12:31-13:13/Galatians 5:22). You see, Corinth had many spiritual manifestations, but they had some major Scorpions as well.

Please note, I didn't say we should leave studying and gifting behind, but that there is a more excellent way to walk in them. Character doesn't come easily and it doesn't come by correct theology or spiritual manifestations. If it did, the church of Corinth would have been a spiritual giant! Instead they had division, strife, sexual sin, and self-appointed apostles.

Consider this: If we are dealing with a scorpion, we will not find it blatantly saying, "I am out to usurp the authorities that be!" Instead, the Scorpion often believes himself to be sincere and on a heavenly mission; the one infected may actually believe that the Scorpion's actions are love-motivated. That is why it is called deception. Usually it is not love motivated, but "right" motivated. The posture of being *right* is more important than the relationship with leaders and others.

Another powerful aspect of the deception is that in some area or technicality, the Scorpion *is* right. But being right technically and having a need to be right can be detrimental to any relationship. One key aspect to a religious attitude (or spirit) is that it possesses an attitude of "rightness" instead of righteousness. Rightness comes from egoism and the satisfaction of being right. Righteousness comes from relationship and the internal rest of being connected. After all, through our *relationship* with Jesus Christ we are made righteous, not the other way around. An attitude of rightness is more concerned with being correct *than being connected.*

Yet, most Scorpions respond with a statement like,

"I walk in love toward people. The reason I'm opposing the minister is because I want people to know the truth." Although the issue at hand may have elements of truth, one key way to discern a Scorpion is in the kind of relationships he or she has. *(Remember, you do not need fruitful relationships to be gifted or biblically intellectual.)* This is the difference between living in a desert and living in the rivers of Living Water. Godly character produces long-lasting, interactive relationships that bring accountability and teachability to everyone. When we do not have true biblical relationships, we have resigned ourselves to religious gymnastics. In other words, when a person does not live in godly character, he has resigned himself to thinking that he will mature by self-centered efforts, like being theologically correct all the time, or being prophetic and being able to see the issues of others.

Above all, Scorpions love attention. But true life in the Spirit is not found in merely being present at church and conventions. It is not found in our spiritual exercises or knowledge. *It is found in close, transparent relationships with members of the Body of Christ with true "biblical" accountability to local church leadership.* If you cannot bear fruit in what you have sown in prayer, study, and **relationship,** you haven't touched the character of God.

> *"For by one Spirit we were all baptized into one body — whether Jews or Greeks, whether slaves or free — and have all been made to drink into one Spirit*
> *(1 Corinthians 12:13/NKJV.")*

"Obey those who rule over you, and be submissive, for they watch out for your souls, as those who must give account. Let them do so with joy and not with grief, for that would be unprofitable for you."

(Hebrews 13:17/NKJV)

As you can see, besides being baptized in water and the Holy Spirit, we are also to be baptized (immersed) in the collective Body (the Church), and we need to be submitted to its leaders. This is where a key aspect of the problem lies: many are trying to *be spiritual,* finding themselves at Bible studies and conferences *independent* from their local church. If a person is involved with this kind of independence, they could be in *Scorpion Pass.* Think about it. According to the Apostle Paul, one of the greatest forms of discipline a local church can exercise toward a person is to remove them from fellowship (1 Corinthians 5:3-7). If that be the case, then why would a believer want to be spiritually allied to a person or persons who does not have any *solid connection* to a local church?

When a person has been removed from close fellowship and accountability in the local church, they have become an open target for Satan (the Scorpion) and his dealings. In the same manner, if we, as believers, remove ourselves from the relationship of the local church, we are pronouncing the same decree on ourselves, making ourselves open targets.

Many times people do this and don't even realize

it. Sometimes it's because they have a need to be special or they have been hurt. In such cases they are using their need or their pain as an excuse. They may stay at home and watch Christian television, which is okay, but it's not a replacement for God's design: connected relationships to the local Church. Fellowshipping in a church is not always the easiest thing to do, *but it is the most profitable.* When people in the church really know you, you can't slip into error very easily. You can't go off and sin without somebody knowing there's something wrong with you or the way you're acting. You can't live carnally, act nastily or proudly, without a good friend coming up to you and telling you the truth. So, in addition to all the prayer and study you give yourself to, you must commit yourself to healthy relationships within the local church. *If not you will become a desert!*

When you are a functioning part of a local church, you will produce wonderful fruit. For this fruit to be seen, you have to exercise love and patience with the immature and carnal. You have to exercise joy, peace and faithfulness when things do not appear well at church and the pastor asks everybody to join in and believe God. You have to be gentle and kind when you instruct the young in the Lord. You have to be drenched in meekness and temperance as you interact with all the different parts of the fellowship. In reality, it takes personal *growth* and *maturity* to be a functional member of the Body of Christ.

The challenge before us, however, is that attaining this character will cost us. It will cost us by no longer allowing ourselves to coddle our pain and/or selfish need. But no, not for the self-made Christian! It's a lot easier to isolate ourselves and not develop the fruit of the Spirit. It's a lot easier NOT to maintain close, transparent, accountable relationships in the church. It's simply a lot easier to open ourselves up to the scorpion! It's a lot easier to be God's "special sheep" who gets all the attention. It's a faster way to be named the "special minister" who only understands the deeper ways of the Spirit. It's a faster way to attain personal recognition among others by having "our own" meetings. When such potential scorpions are confronted by mature Christians, the sad song begins. "They don't understand MY calling..." Or, "I'm being persecuted because of MY unusual gifting and will have to minister to those who will come to my home..." Or here's the big one, "...only God understands ME. No one else ever understands the depth of MY revelations."

One of the main reasons people isolate themselves from healthy relationships in the congregation is because they have been hurt by fellow believers. This is, of course, totally understandable, yet dangerous. Another reason is that they have been confronted by leadership to correct an issue in their life and rather than deal with the problem, they run. When a person runs, in most cases, you can see the larva of a scorpion forming. You begin to hear statements like (said with a whining voice), "Oh, the last church I went to, THEY ALL treated me like an outcast," or, "Oh, the pastor of the last church I went to would NEVER listen to what the Lord was showing me." Followed by (said with a deep sense of purpose), "It has been prophesied over me that many wouldn't understand me, because of my gift...so I had to leave," or, "I had to start this special prayer meeting. Our church leaders would have NEVER understood what I was saying." Here's the clincher (weeping), "All I wanted to do was help and THEY wouldn't let me." It is very rare that such statements are true. Usually these are symptoms of scorpion larva developing.

Such statements remind me of a fellow in the Old Testament named Rehoboam.

> *"Then King Rehoboam consulted the elders who stood before his father Solomon while he still lived, and he said, 'How do you advise me to answer these people?' And they spoke to him, saying, 'If you will be a servant to these people today, and serve them, and answer them, and speak good words to them, then they will be your servants forever.' But he rejected the advice which the elders had given him, and consulted the young men who had grown up with him, who stood before him. And he said to them, 'What advice do you give? How should we answer this people who have spoken to me, saying, 'Lighten the yoke which your father put on us?" Then the young men who had grown up with him spoke to him, saying, "Thus you should speak to this people who have spoken to you, saying, 'Your father made our yoke heavy, but you make it lighter on us' — thus you shall say to them: 'My little finger shall be thicker than my father's waist!*

*And now, whereas my father put a heavy yoke
on you, I will add to your yoke; my father
chastised you with whips, but I will chastise
you with scourges!'" (1 Kings 12:6-11/NKJV)*

In the New International Version it says,
*"Rehoboam **rejected** the advice the elders gave..."*
Rehoboam decided to be different. He wasn't going to
be accountable to the elders and possess a
submissive heart. Instead, he was going to show how
powerful he was. He was going to do his own thing
and impress his peers by heeding their counsel. **He
was going to strike the people like a scorpion.**
In the Hebrew language the word *scorpion* is עַקְרָב
(aqrav), which means "scourge." The scourge was
one of the most feared forms of discipline ever. When
a person was scourged, they were either hung from
the wrists by a rope with their feet almost touching
the ground, or they were tied to a tree stump and
bent over it so they couldn't move. Then the
punisher, or executioner, would take a whip which
was usually knotted with sharp hooks made of metal,
glass or bone, and would strike the victim repeatedly.
The hooks would stick into the flesh and in order to
remove them, the punisher would pull on the whip,
ripping and tearing the flesh off of the body. This was
usually done until the person passed out or died.
They were then left bleeding in that position for the
rest of the day. Keep in mind that after Jesus was
betrayed by Judas, Jesus was *scourged.* In other
words, the Scorpion had struck!

Rehoboam became a Scorpion to the people of
God by not heeding the elders. One of the reasons he

became one was because he felt a threat to his authority. He was afraid of being overthrown by another Scorpion called Jeroboam (more on him in the next chapter).

Whenever we do not have strong roots within ourselves (the making of Godly Character), we open the door for our insecurities to get the best of us, like Rehoboam did. It was out of his insecure, selfish need that he abused God's people. Instead, we need to be rooted with positive, fruit-filled behavior in our relationships. We must have an understanding of whom and what we are as individuals. People who refuse to relate to church leadership and to its people, will either withdraw from almost everyone or elevate themselves. Both rebel against God's design for the local church. When a person has a need to elevate themselves to feed or to deny their insecurity, they will create a Scorpion Pass. This will stunt the growth of what little roots they have. It will make them susceptible to offense and will cause them to become easily embittered at the time of conflict. Keep in mind, we all need well-watered soil to grow deep roots, and **the quality of "fruit" we bear is based on the depth of "root" we have.**

> *"Once more a remnant of the house of Judah will take root below and bear fruit above." (2 Kings 19:30/NIV)*

The principle is that you must take "root" below, to bear "fruit" above.

> *"These likewise are the ones sown on stony*

ground who, when they hear the word, immediately receive it with gladness; and they have no root in themselves, and so endure only for a time. Afterward, when tribulation or persecution arises for the word's sake, immediately they stumble."

(Mark 4:16-17/NKJV)

Offense is perpetual unforgiveness. Unforgiveness is a terrible sin. Unforgiveness is unlike fornication or stealing. When you are done with those type of sins, you can cry out to God in repentance for forgiveness. Unforgiveness is not that obvious. Unforgiveness is like a person in the middle of the act of adultery, looking up to heaven saying, "God forgive me," and continuing with the act for days, weeks, months and even years. I know that sounds vile, but offense or unforgiveness is just that way. It is a constant act, twenty-four hours a day, seven days a week, fifty two weeks a year. It is subtle, quietly working away at one's spiritual life with no evidence until it's too late.

It would be absurd to steal a watch and ask God to forgive you as you walk out of the store with it. In order to truly repent, you would first have to stop shoplifting and then ask God to forgive you. Then, if you truly repented, you would take this a step further. If it's possible, you should return what you stole. In the same manner, it doesn't matter how many times you ask God to forgive you for harboring offenses. **If you don't forgive the person who offended you, you are living in perpetual sin and eventually you will find that you are spiritually stuck!**

"If I had not confessed the sin in my heart, the Lord would not have listened."
(Psalms 66:18/NLT)

"And whenever you stand praying, if you have anything against anyone, forgive him, that your Father in heaven may also forgive you your trespasses. But if you do not forgive, neither will your Father in heaven forgive your trespasses." (Mark 11:25-26/NKJV)

If you are living in unforgiveness, forgive the person who has offended you, thus stopping your sin, and then ask for cleansing and forgiveness from God.

In short, **the Scorpion is formed in an individual who *chooses* not to stay in healthy relationships with people and leadership.** When we resist healthy relationships there is only one alternative: unhealthy ones. Bitterness, by dictionary definition, is: *exhibiting intense animosity with harsh complaints marked by cynicism and rancor* (Merriam-Webster: Dictionary and Thesaurus, 2008). The negative fruit of offense and unforgiveness is bitterness. The product of bitterness is resistance to developing the character of God.

In practical terms, bitterness doesn't start out as sinister as it sounds. Many times people become bitter from conflict, telling themselves they are "fine" and denying that they have a problem. Sometimes they convince themselves that God gave them the revelation to be isolated, when actually it was their own inner deception. Many times when they are in this state of being, the inner voice they call God is really their hurt inner man. Keep in mind that they will attend church and different group meetings. But for them to foster or maintain a relationship, they must have control. They must have supremacy because they must protect their pain and protect themselves from being hurt again. Another strong symptom is that they will always have the answer to their own problems as well as the problems of others. *They must always have the last word!*

In summary, a Scorpion's mode of operation is to entice the weak by demonstrating his gifts and trying to impress others with his knowledge. He infects them with his offenses and passes on his bitterness. The Scorpion grabs his victim through the claws of sympathy or the seduction of flattery. He then vomits his negative digestive juices upon the innocent.

As a Scorpion matures, he usually leaves the people he's associated with emotionally whipped and ready for infection to set in. If a victim tries to end the relationship fostered with a Scorpion, he's told he just wasn't spiritual enough, or is about to walk into some kind of dark spiritual error. This is done in the same manner as the conclusion of the mating ritual; those who try to flee and aren't fast enough are devoured by condescending, condemning, verbal abuse. On the other hand, those maintaining such a relationship wind up with the same seeds of pride and arrogance.

When a Scorpion has had a really successful mission, an entire church can become a Scorpion

Pass. *Because of the pride and arrogance spawned throughout the congregation, split after split after split can occur.*

CHAPTER 2

SEEKING AND STRIKING ITS PREY: THE SHEEP

PART 1: INFILTRATION

"Then Solomon's servant, Jeroboam the son of Nebat, an Ephraimite from Zereda, whose mother's name was Zeruah, a widow, also rebelled against the king. And this is what caused him to rebel against the king: Solomon had built the Millo and repaired the damages to the City of David his father. The man Jeroboam was a mighty man of valor; and Solomon, seeing that the young man was industrious, made him the officer over all the labor force of the house of Joseph." (1 Kings 11:26-28/NKJV)

If there's anything about God's plan Satan fears the most, it is **unity within the local church.** In every biblical instance of united prayer and worshipful harmony among God's people, the powers of darkness were sure to suffer. If you consider Jesus' prayer in the Gospel of John in chapter 17, unity in His Body is the key to the world believing He was sent. In that light, in spite of all the issues of sin and temptation the devil would like to afflict the believer with, division is his decisive tool. When Solomon started to repair the breaches in the city of David (which is symbolic of spiritual restoration and reunification), the devil didn't waste any time with his attack. He sent a prime example of a Scorpion named Jeroboam to Solomon.

In the last chapter we discussed that in Hebrew, the word scorpion is translated, *scourge.* Guess what? Jeroboam's mother was Zeruah צְרוּעָה**,** an Ephrathite of Zereda צְרֵדָה**.** Notice that both words are similar in Hebrew. This can mean they belong to the same family root. צְרוּעָה (tserooah) means *leprous.* Those who had the disease were considered outcasts by the children of Israel. The word implies that one is *stricken* with leprosy. Leprosy in scripture is also considered a spiritual symbol of one who is contaminated with sin. צְרֵדָה (tsereydah), was the place from which Zeruah came, and in Hebrew it means, to *pierce* or *puncture.* When you put the ideas together you would say, *pierced with leprosy.* Consequently, both words come from צָרַע (tsaw'rah) which is none other than *scourge.* The idea is that *one has been pierced with the scourge of leprosy.* The scripture is telling us that Zeruah was afflicted with the scourge (scorpion) of sin.

Well, momma scorpions give birth to baby scorpions and baby scorpions can grow up to be big and strong! Here is a good example of a maturing Scorpion. While King Solomon was trying to fulfill the vision God gave him, in walks "Mr. Capable",

Jeroboam.

He appears to be a pastor's dream: a man of valor, insight, creativity, ambition, and definitely a leader. "Wow," one would think, "He (or she) could be an answer to prayer!" But this is exactly what the Scorpion wants you to believe. He really wants the pastor to think that he is going to bless God's work. But he has another agenda: HIS OWN MINISTRY, HIS OWN WORK, AND THE SHEEP!

Remember something. It doesn't take any spiritual effort in personal character for someone to come into a ministry and claim they are called to a position of authority or influence. All they need is the vulnerability of the sheep. The sheep become vulnerable when leaders allow newcomers into positions of power before they have proven themselves. That's right, *PROVE THEM!* If a man or woman tells you they are called to your church and feels led of God to assist in an area of ministry, don't hand over your Master Card! What I mean is, don't let them near the sheep in any type of position until they have proven loyalty to God and His people. It is totally scriptural to say to that person, "Fine, prove yourself!"

> *"But let these also first be tested; then let them serve as deacons, being found blameless." (1 Timothy 3:10/NKJV)*

Notice it said, *"then let them..."* It did not say to prove them "while" they are in the office of a deacon. I have spoken to pastors who told me of deacons (or elders) that were trouble, but couldn't understand why. These newly found leaders seemed to do so well, but then they became contentious and contrary. The reason is quite simple: they needed to be proven long before they ever had access to a position.

The other problem is in the manner of proof. Most of the time, we read the scriptures in the third chapter of 1 Timothy and only look for those obvious credentials. You know the ones: not a drunkard, husband of one wife, and so on. But there are other provings in this chapter that seem to go unmentioned, even though they're in every verse. They are hidden in each of these scriptures such as, "... husband of one wife..." or "...self-controlled..." They are the concepts of *consistency* and *loyalty*.

> *"For to this end I also wrote, that I might put you to the test, whether you are obedient in all things." (2 Corinthians 2:9/NKJV)*

A man who is *obedient in all things* is a man who will be loyal. Jeroboam was insightful, charismatic with the people, and he appeared to show a genuine concern for the project. But it's safe to say that Jeroboam did not prove himself with loyalty. Instead, he lifted his hand against the king.

In many cases, Christians come into a church feeling the call of God and are hungry to step into ministry. Being called and eager to serve is all well and good, but pastors and leaders need to know if these individuals will be consistent and loyal. The feelings of "need" for a ministry cause pastors, in many cases, to move people into position too soon.

If all you told the eager Jeroboam was to enjoy the presence of the Lord in the assembly and wait on God to speak not only to him, but also to leadership before moving him into position, that would be enough. Yet, if you see him after church pulling people aside, trying to be "the minister" and sharing his ideas on what "should" be done in the church, you could have a potential Scorpion on your hands. One thing is for sure: he's not being submissive, not being relational, not being obedient, and not being self-controlled. If you confront such a person, and their response to you is something like, "God gave me a word for them and you don't want me to be disobedient to God, do you?" watch it! There could be a pair of claws about to grab an innocent lamb.

You may have somebody who is trying to manipulate your authority by putting the responsibility on God for his defiance. That's a good indication this person has no idea what relationship and authority mean. Remind such a one that the Word of God says in the book of Hebrews, *"Obey them that have the rule over you..."* Tell him that the Holy Spirit was present when the book of Hebrews was written, as well as when you told him to sit and not to minister yet. Most of the time, people influenced by the spirit of the Scorpion are looking for an easy ride in ministry (but the spirit itself is looking to destroy the people of God). They want you to labor and build the church so they can come in, drawing attention to themselves by revealing the flaws of the members and the church authority.

After you have corrected Mr. Jeroboam, he will probably look for someone to flex his spiritual muscles toward. You need to realize you have violated the very thing that keeps him feeling good about himself and feeding his ego. Without arrogantly ministering to the innocent, Mr. Jeroboam has nothing left in himself but insecurity and fear. He will most likely seek out someone he has been ministering to and begin to vent his bitterness (in a caring way, of course).

Remember how a scorpion eats? It waits for the innocent creature to approach, then lunges forward, grabbing it with its claws. In other words, this self-proclaimed prophet, preacher, and leader entices Irma[MA8] Innocent to give him a call and ask how things are going. He will then seize this as a feeding opportunity for his ego. Grabbing the person emotionally, he begins with, "God has really been speaking to me about you..." (After the scorpion grabs its victim, it then vomits its digestive juices on its prey.) He continues, "You know, God has been speaking to me about the church too, but the pastor doesn't seem to recognize it. I find it interesting that most of the pastors I know don't recognize what God is trying to say to them." Or perhaps he will say, "I really love our pastor, but I don't think he realizes what's going on spiritually in this matter."

Irma Innocent is then put in a position of responding to the statement. She might say, "Oh, what has God been saying to you? If He's speaking to you, then tell me! I don't want to miss God's will!" Or, "I really love our pastor, too. How can I help?" Well,

Irma just got clawed and she is about to be vomited on. If she questions the Scorpion in a challenging way, he will attack some weak area of her life, proving his supposed superiority. In short, if the victim squirms it will be stung with the unseen poisonous tail.

Leadership needs to teach the members of their congregation to beware of such talk! They need to instruct them that holiness is not only being patient with a slow cashier, or living a celibate life before you're married. *Holiness is also not allowing an accusation about an elder in the Lord to come into your ears!*

"Do not receive an accusation against an elder except from two or three witnesses."
(1 Timothy 5:19/NKJV)

"Do not entertain an accusation against an elder unless it is brought by two or three witnesses." (1 Timothy 5:19/NIV)

"Do not listen to an accusation against an elder unless it is confirmed by two or three witnesses." (1 Timothy 5:19/NLT)

In all three translations of this verse there is a very clear communication to the saints of God. "Do not **receive, entertain** or **listen to..."** This Scorpion spirit would like to infect God's people with its poison in order to make them *witnesses* of the pastor's or leader's error. **The thing is, if the sheep won't listen, he can't succeed.** But if they do listen, then they have been vomited on! If that happens, the innocent lambs will begin to entertain thoughts of doubt and distrust toward the leadership. The only recourse for the lambs is to wash themselves in repentance and tell the leadership what's been going on.

If a lamb has been vomited on with the Scorpion's digestive juice of bitterness and accusation, they will begin to dissolve spiritually. If the individual keeps heeding the Scorpion's words, they will be sucked into a dry spiritual husk. Bitterness is a very ugly thing. It is like cancer of the soul. What's worse is that it can be contagious if we aren't careful. Like cancer, bitterness eats away at its victim little by little. If a person has been vomited on by a Scorpion and receives the foul words, the bitter talk will erode the faith and loyalty of the individual. Ultimately this is not only about faith and loyalty to the church. Once deception sets in, whether he realizes it or not, he is also violating his faith and loyalty to God by placing his trust in the Scorpion.

"See to it that no one misses the grace of God and that no bitter root grows up to cause trouble and defile many." (Hebrews 12:15/NIV)

When a person has been heeding the spiritual garbage the Scorpion has been telling them, it creates a spiritual atmosphere for dependency and allegiance. When Korah (in Numbers 16) told the men of Israel that Moses was not being the leader he should be and that he, himself, had a better way of doing things, it enticed them to follow Korah. A lot of times, leaders like Moses take the people of God through necessary wilderness situations. That's all part of the Church experience. But during these wilderness journeys, people get discontented, uncomfortable, and irritated. This makes them susceptible to "the easy way out." So when a Korah or a Jeroboam-type comes with answers to ease their stress, if they don't understand God's way, they will listen and rebel.

Although you may call the people who follow gullible or blind, in God's eyes they are just as guilty. When the judgment of God came in the situation with Korah, the earth split open and consumed them all. They were all infected with a lethal disease called *insurrection.* When a person listens to and believes the evil lies of a Scorpion, they've become infected with insurrection and if they don't repent, they will be dealt with in the same manner as the Scorpion.

God is a just God, and in the same way He judges the leader, He judges the follower. When Satan fell and took one third of the angels with him (Rev. 12:4,7-9), God judged them all guilty. God didn't say, "Oh, the poor angels, they were so misled! I can't hold them accountable for what happened." He was very clear that their fate was sealed. In like manner according to Jesus, fallen Man will have the same end as Satan and his angels (Matthew 25:41). If Man follows Satan, knowingly or not, he will bear the same judgment. When one follows a Scorpion, his end will also be judged in the same way. Ignorance does not excuse anyone; only repentance and forgiveness do.

When a Scorpion strikes, it will rarely strike

someone who it thinks will figure out what it's doing. Usually, it strikes those it feels can be enticed with little problem. It entices with scriptural knowledge, maybe a dynamic personality, and some spiritual gifts, but at the end of those lures is manipulation and control. Keep in mind that if the victim tries to squirm in the talons of the scorpion, the vicious tail swings from behind, stinging and paralyzing the prey. Would-be Minister Jeroboam says, "You're right Sister Irma, let's not talk about this any longer. We should get some people together and pray for our pastor. I also know you've been having problems in your prayer life, so this will help you as well as the pastor."

Can you imagine what would happen if this Scorpion is not dealt with? Even worse, can you imagine if this Scorpion is given a position of authority in the people's eyes? Perish the thought! If people went to such a prayer meeting, they would definitely be stung by the time they finished. Mr. Scorpion would have them praying, then he would give them some "spiritual" counsel and probably set a time for the next meeting. Irma Innocent, Harry Harmless, Ida Ignorant, and Ollie Oblivious have now become infected if they don't repent. If necessary, they may need to confess their backbiting and gossiping to the congregation. Non-repented followers will become Scorpions themselves. It is inevitable.

The Bible said that Jeroboam lifted up his hand against the king. That's exactly what this demon wants to happen; to have the people of God question and doubt God's men and women in leadership.

"Their talk is foul and filthy like the stench from an open grave. Their tongues are loaded with lies. Everything they say has in it the sting and poison of deadly snakes. Their mouths are full of cursing and bitterness. They are quick to kill, hating anyone who disagrees with them."
(Romans 3:13-15/TLB)

The Scorpion's entire existence is based upon spreading bitterness. The only way it can eat or survive is to vomit up pungent information, making itself grandiose, because it knows something the hearer doesn't.

"The boundary of the Amorites was from Scorpion Pass to Sela and beyond."
(Judges 1:36/NIV)

Those who inhabited Scorpion Pass were the Amorites.

In Hebrew the word אֱמֹרִי (emoriy) "Amorite" means, *sayers* or *publicity.* Its root, אָמַר (amar) means *to say.* The people who live in Scorpion Pass survive by publicizing all the unpleasantness they can find. That's a nice way of saying **they are gossipers!** The Bible also says they lived in Sela and beyond. The word סֶלַע (cela) "Sela" means *a high rocky cliff,* in other words, *to be lofty.* Thus, such people have lifted themselves up in the eyes of those who would listen. In some cases, they even go beyond that and demand blind obedience or pronounce fearsome judgment on those who no longer wish to listen.

I remember a woman who came to the church I pastor and asked me for advice. She told me that a woman prophet who had her own ministry told her that if she were to go to any church other than the one approved by the prophet, she would be in sin and deception. This put a lot of fear in her heart! It didn't bless her or cause her to enter into greater liberty in her relationship with Christ. Instead, it caused her to doubt in her ability to hear the voice of God, and it caused her to waver in decision making. Although she attends our Sunday services once in a while, she never seems to grow or experience change in her life. She is gripped with an innate fear because she was stung by a Scorpion and still remains under the influence of its poison. In short, she has been spiritually paralyzed. This woman should be able to attend her church, visit a friend's church and receive from God, but she can't. In the back of her mind, whether she is in church or listening to a teaching on CD, she is in uncertainty unless she is where the prophetess tells her. This explains the idea of being lofty. The person who told her this elevated herself in the eyes of the woman and created a blind loyalty to capitalize on her insecurities.

In the ministry of Paul, the Apostle, he contended with a major Scorpion at Corinth. Over the years, I've heard and read that Paul's thorn in the flesh was, among other things, an eye disease or anxiety for the churches. Although I am open to any concrete historical proof regarding the possibility of these, much of church history proves these views to be weak. There is no archaeological documentation that says Paul had any kind of disease. As far as him having anxiety because of the churches, this appears to be true at times, but in proper perspective. The one thing we all can agree on, is that the Bible says Paul's thorn was a messenger of Satan, ἄγγελος σατανα (angelos Satana), an angel of Satan. Keep in mind what Jeroboam did, "...he lifted up his hand against the king."

Let me give you another example. Several years ago at a pastors' meeting, I met a wonderful man of God who told a story I will never forget. He said that he went on a missionary journey overseas for a period of weeks, and left the church in the charge of his son-in-law who was his associate pastor. When he returned, he found that church attendance had dropped almost in half. While questioning what happened, he discovered that the associate/son-in-law had taken half the church across town to start his own ministry. The Scorpion strikes again!

Like Jeroboam, the Scorpion-influenced associate gained the favor of the people and then lifted his hand against the senior pastor. Can you imagine what that felt like? After giving most of your life toward building a work for God, half is taken by a demonically influenced person in a matter of weeks. On top of that, this person had gained your trust so closely that you had given your daughter to him in marriage. Your heart would break! Not only because of the betrayal of your son-in-law and daughter, but because sheep you love were deceived and headed for destruction. The end of the story was that the man of God forgave and released his former associate as well as the people who left with him. By doing this, he was able to continue building the work of God in the United States and still plant and reap a harvest overseas. Thank you, Lord Jesus! This pastor chose to forgive instead of becoming embittered.

PART 2: THE STING
PAUL'S THORN IN THE FLESH

It seems that every minister and ministry will come in contact with the spirit of the Scorpion at one time or another. The question is, what is the remedy and the preventive medicine for such a vicious creature? One strong remedy is found in the Apostle Paul's response to the church at Corinth, which had become Scorpion infested. Paul said, "*...there was given to me a thorn in the flesh...*" (2 Corinthians 12:7). The idea of a "thorn in the flesh" is nothing new to the scripture. Paul was using an Old Testament idiom to describe his situation and reveal the wiles of the enemy. Judges 2:3 reveals that people are the thorn, "*... but they shall be as **thorns** in your sides...*" You will find that Paul's thorn is certain people who have spoken against him and his ministry.

Judges 8:7 says, "*...I will tear your flesh with the **thorns** of the wilderness...*" Remember, one definition for the Scorpion is *scourge.* The scourge tears the flesh off those being whipped. The Scorpion stings and poisons its victim, then tears its flesh with its claws. Tearing the flesh with thorns is a very good example of Scorpion activity. In Joshua 23:13, besides having thorns in the eyes, it says, "*... but they shall be...* **scourges** *in your sides...*" The "thorn in the flesh" (the scourge in the side) the Apostle Paul was referring to was people who were spiritually influenced to afflict and torment his leadership.

In the Greek language, the word *scorpion* is σκορπίος (skorpios). It means *to pierce with a stinger.* In other words, it refers to what the scorpion does. For that matter, the base word for scorpion is, σκοπός (skopos) which means, *to peer about, a skeptic;* here is where we get the expression, "He is scoping you out." It is the idea of looking something over with *the attitude of doubt* (Merriam/Webster's Dictionary, skepticism). Lastly it refers to how one does this negative "scoping out." It is kin to the word, σκάπτω (skapto) which means *to dig,* or *to be concealed, hidden.* Thus the word scorpion has these related meanings: **to pierce with the sting of skepticism, injecting the attitude of doubt in a concealed or hidden manner** (in our case, regarding our leaders and church vision).

Sting is another powerful word. It is κέντρον (kentron) which means, *to prick like a thorn, to poison,* or *goad.* Thus, not only does it pierce or prick, but it poisons. The fact that the word *goad* is a definition (according to Thayer's Lexicon), tells us even more about what is going on. Goad means, *to urge into action.* Many times the Scorpion's sting goads or urges its victim into action against leadership. On many occasions I have seen that the Scorpion lies hidden, while those he or she has poisoned do the dirty work and create insurrection.

When people speak evil or gossip about leadership, it is like being pricked with thorns. If such talk goes unchecked, it could end with mutiny or insurrection.

In both books to the Corinthians, several times Paul addresses a particular group of so-called ministers who seem to consistently challenge his ministry and gifting as an apostle. By the time we get to the second epistle, we find these people being sarcastically called "super-apostles" (2 Corinthians 12:11/NLT). After instructing the church at Corinth about their divisions and carnality, the Apostle Paul began to deal with this messenger of Satan, the spirit of the Scorpion (the thorn in the flesh).

> *"But with me it is a very small thing that I should be judged by you or by a human court. In fact, I do not even judge myself. ... For though you might have ten thousand instructors in Christ, yet you do not have many fathers; for in Christ Jesus I have begotten you through the gospel. Therefore I urge you, imitate me." (1 Corinthians 4:3, 15-16/NKJV)*

> *"But I will come to you very soon, if the Lord is willing, and then I will find out not only how these arrogant people are talking, but what power they have. For the kingdom of God is not a matter of talk but of power."*
> *(1 Corinthians 4:19-20/NIV)*[MA9]

The first thing these men did was spread criticism about Paul. They began to judge him and tried to sway the people's opinions of Paul's motives. The motives of an individual are something few people can see based upon one's actions or words. Because of this, we usually perceive people's motives based on what we believe about them. If a Scorpion can influence members of a ministry or congregation that its leader's motives are tainted, it can quickly destroy the leader and the ministry.

Paul, on the other hand, stood against these accusations and encouraged the people to continue following his ministry. In addition, he promised to confront such men by the power of God and reveal their motives of deception. Here is a good example of what we discussed in the last chapter, *Scorpion Pass*. The Corinthian church was gifted. They had wonderful ministers and the congregation was open to the manifestations of the Spirit. But the one major thing they lacked was love, the key to God's character. *Because of a lack of character, the subtle wiles of the devil were allowed to become the declarations of the people.* These later-to-be-called "super-apostles" (also 2 Corinthians 11:5/NIV), were waiting for the perfect moment to strike the people with doubt and thoughts of insurrection.

It all came to the surface when Paul asked them to keep the financial commitment they made to the ministry a year earlier. Yes, Paul had the same problems many ministers deal with today. Can't you just hear that devil? "He only started this ministry to get our money." "How do we know what he's going to do with our money once we give it to him?" "See, he tells you he loves you, but he has his hand out!" "Man! I've been teaching you at my home for months, and I never asked you for a penny. Now this guy, who you can't even get in touch with when you call, wants your hard earned dollars." "A REAL man of God would ask God for himself and not ask God's people for money."

What a liar the devil is! Can you imagine a man like Paul giving his life for the gospel and having to deal with such accusations? Well, Paul does, and takes the time to address those who were poisoned, explaining why it's just and fair to support his ministry.

> *"Am I not free? Am I not an apostle? Have I not seen Jesus our Lord? Are you not the result of my work in the Lord? Even though I may not be an apostle to others, surely I am to you! For you are the seal of my apostleship in the Lord. This is my defense to those who sit in judgment on me. ... Or is it only I and Barnabas who must work for a living?"*
> *(1 Corinthians 9:1-6/NIV)*

Paul, out of the goodness of his heart, worked as a tent maker and received support from other churches so the Corinthian church wouldn't be burdened at its inception with his expenses. But the Scorpion used Paul's benevolence to its own advantage. When the time came for the people to become responsible for the ministry, this demon tried to make Paul look money-hungry. Unfortunately, the

Scorpion was, to some measure, successful and influenced the people to think critically and carnally. As a result, Paul had to explain the responsibilities of God's people toward the ministry. He specified that just because he didn't ask before, didn't mean they shouldn't give now. He told them that he didn't ask for material blessings in the past because he didn't want their lack of finances to hinder them from receiving the Gospel. He simply asked another church to help with his ministry expenses in Corinth, and worked as a tent maker as well.

"If we have sown spiritual seed among you, is it too much if we reap a material harvest from you? If others have this right of support from you, shouldn't we have it all the more? But we did not use this right. On the contrary, we put up with anything rather than hinder the gospel of Christ." (1 Corinthians 9:11-12/NIV)

Men and women of God, one way to destroy the works of the devil is to support God's leader financially!

"For the love of money is the root of all evil: which while some coveted after, they have erred from the faith, and pierced themselves through with many sorrows."
(1 Timothy 6:10.KJV)

If you want to *destroy* the root of all evil and keep yourself from being *pierced* with the sting of the Scorpion, fall in love with the work of God and **GIVE!** *Giving will destroy the roots of satanic activity.* When we give, we are taking the strength of our labors and sowing it to another. By doing this we empower others to serve and we manifest God's character. Satan, however, would love to accuse God's leader so he will not be empowered to act on behalf of the Kingdom.

As God's leader, when Satan has falsely accused you of motives which are truly not yours, your only defense may be to say like Paul:

"But by the grace of God I am what I am..."
(1 Corinthians 15:10)

Keep this in mind: they were not just attacking Paul's integrity in this situation, they were also attacking the grace of God on his life by judging him.

"For I am the least of the apostles, who am not worthy to be called an apostle, because I persecuted the church of God. But by the grace of God I am what I am, and His grace toward me was not in vain; but I labored more abundantly than they all, yet not I, but the grace of God which was with me.
(1 Corinthians 15:9-10/NKJV)

Paul states that he is an apostle not because those in Corinth approved of him, but by the grace of God [and the affirmation of the council of Antioch and Jerusalem (Acts 9 & 13)]. The bottom-line was that God, not man, gave him the grace of apostleship and it was affirmed by credible ministries. (Please note, I did not say *famous* ministries, I said *credible* ministries.) Paul tells Corinth that the proof of this grace on his life is the Corinthian church itself. The very fact that they existed, had faith in Christ, and could even be in a position to challenge his labors, was proof of Paul's work. Nonetheless, the Scorpion wouldn't stop stinging with accusations and Paul wouldn't paralyze easily. The battle continued.

> *"Do we begin again to commend ourselves? Or do we need, as some others, epistles of commendation to you or letters of commendation from you? You are our epistle written in our hearts, known and read by all men; clearly you are an epistle of Christ, ministered by us, written not with ink but by the Spirit of the living God, not on tablets of stone but on tablets of flesh, that is, of the heart." (2 Corinthians 3:1-3/NKJV)*

Again, in the second epistle to the Corinthian church, Paul states how the grace of apostleship was truly working in him and toward them. He proves to the church that they are a fellowship because of the Holy Spirit working through him and toward them, not because several people on their board voted for him. It was truly because of a genuine gift of God and ministering in the love and character of Christ (even to his own hurt), which brought about the growing church. In other words, Paul didn't establish the church simply with his gifts, but with his character.

> *"Open your hearts to us. We have wronged no one, we have corrupted no one, we have cheated no one." (2 Corinthians 7:2/NKJV)*

"But I beg you that when I am present I may not be bold with that confidence by which I intend to be bold against some, who think of us as if we walked according to the flesh."
(2 Corinthians 10:2/NKJV)

These Scorpion-poisoned people proclaimed that Paul was a man of the flesh, that he wasn't very spiritual, and that his motives were corrupt. (Remember, the Scorpion is always trying to act more spiritual than others.) They said he was not equivalent to their elite religious group with all its special revelations and ideas, and that true spirituality was judged by them, not by Paul. They also tried to demean Paul's strength of character by saying that he was only bold in his letters and not in person. (I guess they never read what happened to Korah when he stood against Moses.)

Beware, men and women of God! This is what the Scorpion is out to do! He is going to try and lure people over into his territory. We can't be foolish like the prophet, Balaam. It was over financial issues that the devil tried to get him to prophesy for his evil purposes. Many times we get angry when we are challenged to give, and due to our own immaturity, fall prey to this evil spirit. On the other hand, if we don't fall prey to the Scorpion's criticism, we may try to battle him with the anger of the flesh and that also leads to destruction. That's what this devil was trying to do to Paul. He was trying to get Paul to flex his spiritual muscles by the anger of the flesh. Satan was saying, "Paul, if you are really the Apostle of God, prove it now. Not just by some boasting letter, but by prophesying against these men who are critical of you."

People of God, if you fall prey to those temptations, you've been bitten by the Scorpion yourself and will wind up as an enemy of God. *You cannot fight the fires of the devil with the burning of the flesh.* You have to destroy the fires of the Scorpion by the cool water of the Holy Spirit. So, instead of lashing out with some spiritual prophecy of doom and gloom, Paul continued to validate his ministry by proven fruit (Godly character), only later to reveal the source of these men's accusations.

It's easy for someone to come into a church where he or she has never labored and to become critical, pointing out error in the leadership. But it's not in Gods character for someone who has labored in the church to validate themselves by pointing out the errors of others, so Paul tells Corinth that he doesn't criticize other men's labors, and that he never boasts of the work someone else has done to his fame or reward. He says that all men's labor should be to the praise and glory of God alone.

"I may seem to be boasting too much about the authority given to us by the Lord. **But our authority builds you up; it doesn't tear you down.** *So I will not be ashamed of using my authority... Those people should realize that our actions when we arrive in person will be as forceful as what we say in our letters from far away. Oh, don't worry; we*

wouldn't dare say that we are as wonderful as these other men who tell you how important they are! But they are only comparing themselves with each other, using themselves as the standard of measurement. How ignorant! We will not boast about things done outside our area of authority. We will boast only about what has happened within the boundaries of the work God has given us, which includes our working with you. We are not reaching beyond these boundaries when we claim authority over you, as if we had never visited you. For we were the first to travel all the way to Corinth with the Good News of Christ. Nor do we boast and claim credit for the work someone else has done. Instead, we hope that your faith will grow so that the boundaries of our work among you will be extended. Then we will be able to go and preach the Good News in other places far beyond you, where no one else is working. Then there will be no question of our boasting about work done in someone else's territory. As the Scriptures say, 'If you want to boast, boast only about the Lord.' When people commend themselves, it doesn't count for much. The important thing is for the Lord to commend them.

(2 Corinthians 8, 10:11-18/NLT)

Paul tells the church that the reason for his authority was not to be a burden to them, but for an increase of their faith and hope. Paul wanted nothing less than to be a real blessing to God's people. He loved the Lord and loved seeing people delivered from sin's hold so much, that he was bold in confronting Corinth's objection. He clearly establishes that he didn't come from a small group of people who only compared themselves to each other. Rather, he was a servant of the entire Body of Christ and was accountable to whole teams of ministry. Paul also brings a wonderful truth to light about spiritual authority when he says *"...we stretch not ourselves beyond our measure..."* He was letting the leaders of Corinth know that he wouldn't invade another person's area of authority because this is offensive to Christ. By his testimony of spiritual ethics, he was also revealing their error.

In short, Paul was saying that these men were never given authority; they hijacked it! On top of their commandeering this authority, they also claimed that the growth of the church was due to their work, and that Paul had no claim in the effort. Basically, they said they didn't need Paul anymore and had outgrown his ministry. Paul responded by saying:

"...when you become stronger in your faith, we will be able to reach many more of the people around you. That has always been our goal." (2 Corinthians 10:15/CEV)

In other words, Paul said, "You didn't outgrow us, but you have enlarged the reach of our ministry." Many times I have heard people say, "I'm not being fed by the pastor anymore. I've outgrown his ministry." No way! If you have grown to a place of maturity where you're living what the pastor is preaching, that means two things. First, you have a good pastor who brought you to that place of maturity. Secondly, it's time to submit to your pastor and elders on a greater level and join their leadership in building the ministry. If you have increased, then so should the church and the Kingdom. People of God, quit looking for sermons and ministers to dazzle you. **Start dazzling your church with your own maturity in godly character!**

Finally, Paul gets down to the issue: money. He tells Corinth that his positive, ethical, and spiritual relationships to other churches made it possible for them to be viable. He clarifies by sharing that he never intended to be a burden, nor would he be in the future, but for them to simply fulfill their pledge.

"I 'robbed' other churches by accepting their contributions so I could serve you at no cost. And when I was with you and didn't have enough to live on, I did not become a financial burden to anyone. For the brothers who came from Macedonia brought me all that I needed. I have never been a burden to you, and I never will be." (2 Corinthians 11:8-10/NLT)

It is not God's best for other ministries to support the gift of God when he or she ministers in your church. One of the greatest problems the church-world has faced is the marketing mailing list. Some ministers have resorted to manipulative marketing in their newsletters to support their traveling efforts. This is one of the main areas where the Scorpion has had an open door to cause either insurrection or strife. It is not wrong for the minister and, in particular, the missionary to ask for support. But because local churches do not always have the resources they need to keep up with their responsibilities, many felt they had to use "worldly" tactics to create the needed finances. The justification for this was based on the unspoken perspective that the end justifies the means. Thus, the Scorpion has struck, accusing those who use such methods and tainting those who desire to give with a fear of giving.

Many missionaries are living at poverty levels for the cause of Christ, which is commendable, but not necessarily God's will! What if the local church wasn't plagued with Western Christian commercialism? Whether we know it or not, many members of the congregation have been paralyzed and have become victims of insurrection because of how Christendom commercially promotes ministry. There is nothing wrong with advertising a new book or CD, but some have been bitten by a Scorpion with a very long-reaching tail and don't even know it.

In addition, the Bible says *"...to know them that labor among you."* It would clearly be more consistent with scripture if every evangelist, traveling minister and missionary had a supporting Church body. But because of the spirit of the Scorpion, true apostolic missionary teams who desire to pioneer new churches have lived at poverty levels when there's more than enough funds available in the Kingdom to meet their needs. A church should send forth their ministries and GIVE them a financial base to work from. In this way, they can spend their time furthering the work of the Gospel instead of praying for their next meal.

Macedonia shouldn't have had to continually support Paul's labor in Corinth. Corinth should have taken responsibility to support his efforts in their community. In other words, when Paul was at Corinth, the members of that church body should have paid for most of his expenses! Not only should they have supported his ministry to them, but they should have sent him to regions beyond. Because they loved Paul and the work of the Lord, they should have sent him out with healthy, "reasonable" support to start new churches, or to bless functioning ones. This may sound unfamiliar to some, but it is the scriptural pattern. In this way, true relationships are built, and called men and women *are not ministering to eat, but ministering to feed.*

Paul then reveals the motivating force behind these so-called Corinthian leaders. He reveals that they are messengers of Satan, trying to stop God's work and poisoning the church.

"For such men are false apostles, deceitful workmen, masquerading as apostles of Christ. And no wonder, for Satan himself masquerades as an angel of light. It is not surprising, then, if his servants masquerade as servants of righteousness. Their end will be what their actions deserve. I repeat: Let no one take me for a fool. But if you do, then receive me just as you would a fool, so that I may do a little boasting." (2 Corinthians 11:13-16/NIV)

These false apostles, as Paul called them, were simply messengers of Satan, masquerading as servants of righteousness. With their accusations, they were trying to get Paul to fight in their arena. Whenever Satan incites a battle, he will always try to get us to respond carnally. It is only in the arena of the flesh that a believer can be conquered. If we walk in Godly character, the devil is no match for us. As Paul said, *"...the weapons of our warfare are mighty through God..."* By not crossing over from Divine character to carnality and choosing not to battle by egoistic defense (boasting and self-glory), Paul was a sure winner. He chose not to be "a fool", but to testify of God's grace on his life instead.

> *"It is doubtless not profitable for me to boast. I will come to visions and revelations of the Lord: For though I might desire to boast, I will not be a fool; for I will speak the truth. But I refrain, lest anyone should think of me above what he sees me to be or hears from me. And lest I should be exalted above measure by the abundance of the revelations, a thorn in the flesh was given to me, a messenger of Satan to buffet me, lest I be exalted above measure.*
> *(2 Corinthians 12:1, 6-7/NKJV)*

Paul could have said, "Hey! Who do you think you are? I've had visions and revelations. I've started many churches and had miracles beyond measure in my ministry. I don't need you to approve of me! Good riddance to you all! You'll never hear from me again!" But he didn't. Instead, he said that if he boasted about the great things God had done in him, it would be the truth, but it wouldn't gain anything for his cause and the cause of Christ. As a matter of fact, if they followed him on the basis of his boasting, he wouldn't want to be exalted in that manner anyway (in their eyes or his own). So false apostles, those who had been under the influence of *the messenger of Satan,* were sent to torment him. They were sent to tempt him to be puffed up and justify himself. But instead it worked in the reverse! Instead of being exalted in the eyes of others and puffed up in his own, he humbled himself and rested in the grace of God. He allowed the grace of God to turn situations around for the best. He allowed the accusations of the enemy to assist him in discovering another depth of humility.

"Three times I pleaded with the Lord to take it away from me. But he said to me, 'My grace is sufficient for you, for my power is made perfect in weakness.' Therefore I will boast all the more gladly about my weaknesses, so that Christ's power may rest on me. That is why, for Christ's sake, I delight in weaknesses, in insults, in hardships, in persecutions, in difficulties. For when I am weak, then I am strong. I have made a fool of myself, but you drove me to it. I ought to have been commended by you, for I am not in the least inferior to the 'super-apostles', even though I am nothing."

(2 Corinthians 12:8-11/NIV)

Paul asked God several times to rid him of the source of this temptation, these so-called "super-apostles", who were under the influence of this messenger of Satan. But God responded with the statement that *His grace* on Paul's life was sufficient and strong enough to survive the attack. The fact that God, by His grace, used Paul to birth this church would be the powerful, sustaining element of proof for the church during this time. In addition to this, the grace would be mighty through God to pull down *the human reasonings* or *arguments* these men were creating.

In Greek the word "stronghold" ὀχύρωμα (ochuroma), literally means *a fortress,* but it was also used by philosophers as a description of *intellectual arguments* (Philo of Alexandria for example). Here in 2 Corinthians 10:3-5/NIV, the Apostle Paul takes up the same usage.

The key to fighting the spirit of the Scorpion is the grace of God upon your life. You do not need to prove yourself by arguing or being "right" in the situation. While Satan was tempting Paul with ego and pride, the very act of this temptation pressed him into humility, the basis for the strength of Christ.

To spiritually cast down the arguments (strongholds) of the enemy that come against you, you must first cast them down within yourself. This is extremely difficult if you believe yourself to be right. This is when the ego, the source of all sin, rises up and says, "I have a right!" But God says, "My grace is sufficient for you, for My strength is made perfect in weakness."

All you have to do is rest in the fact that God's grace is bigger than the opposition, both internally and externally. If it was truly by God's grace that the work was started, then it will be by God's grace that the work continues. You never need to boast about what you've done, because the grace of God will proclaim what He has done. Paul so much as said, *"You call me weak, you insult me, you created hardship by not giving, and you persecute me with difficulties. Fine! When I am weak, the grace of God is my strength!"*

Leader of God, you can glory in your tribulations, because tribulation works patience, and patience remembers its experiences of victory, and that hope will never cause you shame (Romans 5:1-5)!

> *"The things that mark an apostle--signs, wonders and miracles--were done among you with great perseverance. How were you inferior to the other churches, except that I was never a burden to you? Forgive me this wrong!" (2 Corinthians 12:12-13/NIV)*

Once again, Paul did not prove himself to them by boasting, Instead, he simply said to look at his fruit. He expounded that when he was with them, there were signs and wonders of the Holy Spirit, just like in other churches. He showed them that they didn't fall short in any area of spiritual growth, *except one.* In that one place of depravity, he asked them for forgiveness. He recognized that he may have failed them in the area of their financial responsibility toward his ministry. Paul's final statement is his key blow in his offensive strike against the Scorpion.

> *"This will be the third time I am coming to you. 'By the mouth of two or three witnesses every word shall be established.' I have told you before, and foretell as if I were present the second time, and now being absent I write to those who have sinned before, and to all the rest, that if I come again I will not spare – since you seek a proof of Christ speaking in me, who is not weak toward you, but mighty in you. "*
>
> *(2 Corinthians 13:1-3[MA10]/NKJV)*

The final statement that won the battle was that Christ was truly speaking in Paul. This was the irrefutable proof that Christ used Paul's ministry to establish the people in Corinth. The biblical evidence for apostolic ministry is a growing, productive church that can exist without the presence of its founder. The fact that they were saved and were a growing church was Paul's confirmation.

<u>A NOTE TO GOD'S LEADER</u>: One of the major ways to successfully battle and triumph over the spirit of the Scorpion is to rest in God's grace on your life. You have to know that you are called and selected for His purpose. As the scripture declares, *"...make your calling and election sure..."* (2 Peter 1:10). This is where one's personality in Godly character is tempered and revealed. A person seasoned with

Godly character will have the inner confidence and peace to stand his or her ground. The only shallow defense the Scorpion has against this is our ego. Satan doesn't play fair. Neither should we. The posture of a child of God rooted in humility turns the table on darkness, leaving it with a great disadvantage.

On the other hand, there are times when we need to make a humble, yet clear stand, for the sake of the congregation. Don't be afraid to openly rebuke Scorpions if the need arises! You don't even have to single them out by name. All you have to do is reveal them by preaching and teaching Godly accountability and relationship. If necessary, expose the Scorpion by explaining how it works to deceive God's people. In extreme cases, use situations and circumstances that are actually happening; you won't even have to mention any names. Yet, if they don't repent, continuing to poison the sheep, mark them publicly (Romans 16:17-18). Tell the congregation what the Scorpions are doing and command those causing the strife to leave the fellowship.

God, and for that matter His people, are looking for men and women with the kind of character that will be humble, yet strong in battle. God's people want to feel protected by their leaders. In this era, the sheep are looking for leaders of purpose, determination and strength! As a member of my church once said, "We are not in the last days; we are in the last minutes!"

A NOTE TO GOD'S PEOPLE: Don't listen to the

offenses of others! *The Scorpion will die hungry if you don't feed it with your time and ears.* If you have been growing in a church, then rejoice and don't listen to the complaints of others. No one is perfect and that includes your leader! There will be those who will find some garbage in a leader's past, making a mountain out of a mole hill. Just tell those who spread such poison to *BE QUIET!* Tell them to *LEAVE YOU ALONE!* Warn them that if they come near you again, you will march them over to church leadership and *TELL ALL!* Command them not to spread these lies over the Blood-covered past of others and tell them you will be watching if they try!

CHAPTER 3

SEEKING AND STRIKING ITS PREY
- THE PASTOR

I'm sure the examples we've explored so far have revealed either current activity or brought to remembrance situations in the past where a Scorpion was at work. But in all that was unveiled, there is still a more insidious objective to be dealt with: the striking of the pastor.

We have to realize that this kind of spiritual activity does not want to control and possess authority, like some others. The Scorpion is similar to, but not to be confused with, the spirit of Jezebel. In the book of 1 Kings, Jezebel seduced, manipulated, and controlled her husband, King Ahab of Israel. She did this for the purpose of dominating the kingdom *through* him. The Scorpion, however, through its adaptation of manipulation, desires to poison its victims with bitter insurrection[MA11] for the self-serving pleasure of vomiting its egocentric toxins, and drawing people to itself. **If it can get into the good graces of a pastor or ministry leader and infect him with its bitterness, it will ultimately have victory.**

As far as those who dwell in darkness are concerned, the effects would be wonderful. It would leave the pastor striking out at the congregation in frustration and anger. **The Pastor or leader would in effect become a Scorpion!** If possible, the powers of darkness will attempt to frustrate the pastor to the point where he or she will fall into sin. This will result in either resignation or dismissal, hurting the sheep on several levels. (Please keep in mind that every pastor who falls into sin is not necessarily struck by the Scorpion. Many times we in the ministry have traded spiritual maturity for ministry success. The result is devastating. The Scorpion, Jezebel, and Satan just sit on the sidelines enjoying the show.)

Another important fact about the Scorpion is that it doesn't just show up in a ministry because it feels like attacking it. The fact is (from a spiritual point of view) it was living in that region for a long time, keeping the people in dryness and from walking in the rivers of Living Water. So even though you may have a new person or even a new believer causing the problem, *the spirit influencing them* has been around and at work for a long time. Not only is this an issue within the local church, but it can be a symptom of something on a broader scale. When churches have difficulty unifying with other ministries, this could be an indication that the community is a Scorpion Pass. Keep in mind that this creature is usually quite patient as it waits for its food. But it will viciously sting and devour anything that threatens it. Unity, in both the local church and the community, is considered a threat.   After all when we gather together in Christ's Name, anything is possible! (Matthew 18:20).

One of the biggest threats on the Scorpion's life is **unity** among and in churches with a vision to see their city touched by God. By desiring this, you have changed its relatively dry, desert-like habitat into spiritually wet soil, which, when sown with the seed of the Gospel, will bear much fruit. Don't think for a moment the Scorpion will just allow you to do this. It will come at you with its clippers and stinger swinging. You must really be making progress in your ministry and your city for that kind of response. The Scorpion knows you have been receiving from the waters of God's Spirit and it wants you dry. Its goal is to taint your ability to receive from God so it can hinder or even destroy the Divine product. *But don't fear! If God didn't think you could handle it, you wouldn't be where you are with that kind of mission!*

"Yes, my father laid heavy burdens on you, but I'm going to make them even heavier! My father beat you with whips, but I will beat you with scorpions!" (1 Kings 12:11/NLT)

As we said earlier, King Rehoboam was under the influence of the Scorpion and was going to afflict God's people as a result. The difference between Jeroboam and Rehoboam was that Jeroboam was the kind of Scorpion that influenced the people against the king (pastor or leader). King Rehoboam, on the other hand, was a leader that the Scorpion influenced *to afflict the people.* **Yes there are those in authority who are Scorpions!** The Bible said that

Rehoboam counseled with the younger men and was swayed by them and *afflicted the people.*

> *"So Rehoboam rested with his fathers, and was buried with his fathers in the City of David. His mother's name was Naamah, an Ammonitess. Then Abijam his son reigned in his place." (1 Kings 14:31/NKJV)*

In the same manner that Jeroboam's ancestry influenced him, so did Rehoboam's. Rehoboam's mother was an Ammonitess. The Ammonites were the children of the incestuous son of Lot. Ammonite עַמּוֹנִי in Hebrew means, "inbred or incest." Incest, how terrible! Remember also that Rehoboam lived in Shechem שְׁכֶם, which in Hebrew means, "the place of burdens." Rehoboam was "burdened" with fears and insecurities about the throne.

> *"Therefore, brothers, try even harder to make your being called and chosen **a certainty**. For if you keep doing this, you will never stumble." (2 Peter 1:10/CJB)*

It is so important to be confident in what you receive from God. I am not referring to an intellectual understanding of scripture about righteousness and forgiveness from sin. I am talking about understanding yourself and your relationship with God. If you are not sure about yourself and the call of God, *the Scorpion will begin to maneuver its way into your good graces, attempting to comfort* [MA15]*your insecurities.*

Every leader has the opportunity to get discouraged but because of that, every leader should have someone (an elder in the Lord), who will speak truth into their lives (born out of a loving relationship). If not, the Scorpion would *lust after such a position.* If you are not careful, it will begin to shrewdly influence your decisions and the way you think. It will try to be your spiritual advisor by preying on your insecurities. *In other words, the mating dance has begun.* Then, when you least expect it, it will grab you with its claws! It will come with much strength and say, "Pastor, we have been working together for awhile and this is laying heavy on my heart. Listen to what God told me to tell you to do..." LOOK OUT! Here it comes! "In a vision the Lord showed me that the church is going to go through a very hard time if you don't do this... or that..." If you are a leader with a heart to serve God, but insecure about the way you serve, you're dead meat at this point. If you even think to yourself, "Well, I'll listen and test it," you're going to get stung.

Men and women of God every leader needs leaders around them who are not "yes men", but honest people who will to tell them the truth. But while they are being honest and maybe even lovingly confrontational, they are still "safe" to be in relationship with. The difference is that Scorpions are not interested in protecting anyone; they are interested in their own agenda!

I remember a few years ago, when I was a guest speaker at a church, a person claimed to be very blessed by the ministry. At least that's what I was supposed to believe. This person called my office and asked to have a counseling appointment with me. I said that we could meet, but as a general rule I don't usually do ongoing counseling with people I do not pastor. The only exception is if their pastor is aware of our meeting and is regularly updated on our progress. I did inform the person that I would give a report to their leadership after the meeting, if there was an issue of significance. (I did call the eldership and informed them of this pending conversation. I told them I would keep them apprised of its outcome, especially if it was consequential.) The moment we sat down to talk, I could sense something was very wrong. The statement that really clued me in was when the person said they were the *"spiritual advisor"* of the *"former pastor"* of their church. At that point, the person began to speak out their bitterness and poison. It wasn't just as if they wanted to reveal a pain so they could be healed. *They were clearly out to anger me with their words* at the current leadership and cause division between us. As soon as the meeting was over (and it was over quickly), I told the elders of the church that this person was hurting and needed some ministry. I also told them that they needed to watch this person closely for a potential problem. Sadly, the church did eventually split and this person was definitely a key part of the problem. **What made it even worse was that this person was correct in many of the issues they were addressing, but their bitterness was so strong, they couldn't bring a solution to the issues at hand.**

Pastor, before you listen to anything, make sure you are secure in God and that you and your eldership have the kind of *healthy* relationship where they are confident in your decisions, though not the "yes men" we spoke of earlier. If you don't and they don't...you're history when the accusations come! You will listen to this person and walk around in fear of the possibility that what's been said is true. But if you are strong in the Lord and in the power of His might, you'll understand what is really going on. The Scorpion is trying to capitalize on your insecurities and maneuver you into an unholy relationship.

Incest is an unholy relationship and this kind of spiritual relationship is incestuous! If God has given you faithful elders, then the people you need to hear are those who are proven in loyalty to God and you; the kind of people whose lives resemble the Word of God and are of a good reputation. In other words, they will tell you what they feel God is saying. They are part of a team working toward the same goal. They are a people who always turn the heart of the sheep to your shepherdship and to the Lordship of Jesus Christ. They are not looking to run the church through you, but desire for Jesus Christ to be Lord of the church. They are submitted and ethical to God, to each other, to you, and to the sheep.

The Scorpion, however, would try to get pastors into a spiritually unholy relationship. Because Rehoboam came from his incestuous forefather, Lot, the whole bloodline was strongly influenced by this deed. Two of the many idols that were worshipped by his children were Molech and Ashtoreth. The spirit of the Scorpion is from the Molech/Ashtoreth family. One of the most famous influences from Ashtoreth (also called Asherah) is Jezebel. Jezebel is acclaimed for her seductive, diabolical manipulation and control of King Ahab. Jezebel was also called a whore and a witch (2 Kings 9:22).

> *"...And bring the four hundred and fifty prophets of Baal and the four hundred prophets of Asherah, who eat at Jezebel's table." (1 Kings 18:19/NIV)*

Molech, on the other hand, was an idol of total destruction and its worship was famous for child sacrifice. Molech was the Phoenician deity of Ammon (or incest).

> *"He followed Ashtoreth the goddess of the Sidonians, and Molech the detestable god of the Ammonites." (1 Kings 11:5/NIV)*

Rehoboam grew up in an environment that did not teach him how to serve the Lord. Instead, Solomon brought him up under the power of the enticing snare of Ashtoreth and incestuous Molech.

According to the dictionary, incest means two closely related people having a sexual act that is forbidden by law, a mother/son relationship for example. Most controlling and manipulative relationships produce incestuous "emotional" behaviors with children. (This is because a child is taught to depend upon the manipulation of the parent or adult, rather than learning to exercise quality choices with a parent's guidance.) Ammon was born by Lot's younger daughter after she had sex with her father. She seduced him by getting him drunk and then *when he was under the influence,* she slept with him. In such a case, whether the child is making advancements to the parent or the parent to the child, it is ultimately still the parent's responsibility to respond appropriately. In the same manner, a leader can never say with any truth, "She (or he) made the advancement to me and I could not help myself." A parent should be guiding a child, not treating them like a spouse. In current terminology, we call this a dysfunctional family. *In bible terminology we call it SIN!* Keep in mind that just because you are not having sex with your children, doesn't mean there isn't an incestuous type of relationship. If a son takes the father's role in a family and "husbands" his mother, that's emotional incest, even if the husband should die and leave the children fatherless! It is appropriate for the oldest brother to take the father-like role to his brothers and sisters, but it is not his job to meet the emotional needs of his mother as her husband (his father) did.

This can also happen in father-daughter relationships, as with Lot and his daughters. Maybe Mom is an alcoholic, or a drug addict, or simply a dreadful wife. Because of the conduct of the mother, it provokes such improper behavior between father and daughter, yet it is still inappropriate! By the time Lot's daughter did her deed with her father, her mother was already a pillar of salt. I do not believe that Lot's daughter would have chosen incest if her mother was around, regardless of the reasons. When an emotional incest ties a parent and a child inappropriately, this could eventually produce a physical act. This is one of the "innocent" or better said, "blind" ways incest can begin. In these types of cases, no incest or abuse may have existed in the background of the parent to spur on the problem with their children. But all of a sudden, they are having sexual feelings for their child. They opened themselves up emotionally to their child in a way they should have never allowed.

This is reminiscent of an evil personality in scripture named, Nimrod. (Nimrod was the fellow who built the tower of Babel and historically attempted to burn Abram and his brother Haran in Ur.) Nimrod was the great-grandson of Noah. Nimrod's grandfather was Ham, who after seeing Noah drunk and naked told his brothers Japheth and Shem (Genesis 9:21-22). His brothers covered their father, but Ham was cursed because he did not cover his father, but exposed him. (Some take this to an extreme saying that Ham had a homosexual encounter with his father, but there is no Biblical or historical evidence to support this whatsoever.)

According to historians, Nimrod and his mother, Sammu-ramat, had an incestuous relationship. She was a self-proclaimed goddess and appears in many pre-Christian religions as the goddess of fertility and sexuality. Some of her many names throughout history are Semiramis, Ishtar, Aset (Isis), and Devaki. She also had a sister who is known in the Old Testament as Ashtoreth, whose worship involved what we call, "temple prostitution." As time went on and the Greco-Roman civilizations emerged, her identity became blurred. She was attributed to Artemis, Aphrodite, Diana and Venus, but none of them were the complete personification of her. Nonetheless, one of her more interesting attributes as it relates to the spirit of the Scorpion is that of Sammu-ramat. She was terrible to her lovers and killed her mates after she had sex with them. The only one she really loved was Nimrod.

As far as the New Testament is concerned, an example of an incestuous relationship is in 1 Corinthians 5:1-8, between a mother (or as some believe, step-mother) and son. To add to the spiritual confusion, the Corinthian religious system (before Christ was introduced to them), also involved temple prostitution, which can be traced to Ashtoreth. The church of Corinth was exhorted to remove the leaven of this sin from the church so it wouldn't spread through the whole Body.

What I'm getting at is this: elders and church leaders should spend their time ministering to the sheep and caring for each other, instead of asking their sheep to govern and pastor the church.

We are all to love each other, but the average church member shouldn't have to carry the burden that the elders carry, especially when it comes to issues with other members and their perils. The Bible doesn't teach hierarchy per se[MA16], but it does teach servant-leadership (Ephesians 4:10). To put it another way, a mother needs to care for her son, and a son needs to care for his mother. The mother and son (or father and daughter), need to have a transparent, honest relationship. But when a mother needs a husband, she'd better leave her son alone, spiritually, emotionally, and physically!

If a church member is not anointed for eldership, or at the very least, not spiritually mature, then don't confide in him as if he is. Confiding in the sheep with church business is like a father confiding things to his daughter that only his wife can really handle. Elders should confide in elders. If a person in the church is called to that position, then take the time to groom them, as Paul did Timothy. Don't promote a person to eldership because they have a revelation or gift (more on that in a later chapter). Ordain them as an elder because they display Godly characteristics and spiritual qualities for that position!

> *"Do not neglect your gift, which was given you through a prophetic message when the body of elders laid their hands on you."*
> *(1 Timothy 4:14/NIV)*

> *"I have been reminded of your sincere faith, which first lived in your grandmother Lois and in your mother Eunice and, I am persuaded, now lives in you also. For this reason I remind you to fan into flame the gift of God, which is in you through the laying on of my hands. For God did not give us a spirit of timidity, but a spirit of power, of love and of self-discipline." (2 Timothy 1:5-7/NIV)*

Notice that the Apostle Paul blessed Timothy, his

son in the faith. He encouraged him to use the gifts he had. But, Paul did not seize the opportunity to capitalize on Timothy's insecurities (or timidity, 2 Timothy 1:7). Instead, he built up Timothy to depend on God. He gave him confidence in what was given by God. Paul was not pursuing Timothy's position or running the church through Timothy! He was in pursuit of Timothy's personal growth and the church's expansion. On the other hand, our over-friendly Scorpion may say, "Oh Pastor, but that's all I want too!" Try again!

Scorpions tell you what they think you want to hear, but their *FRUIT* is another story. So what do we do? **Examine their past histories.** Have they left regular messes behind them at the churches they previously attended? Did they get angry every time they weren't agreed with? Have they bragged about all the great things they've done at the previous churches? Do they say things like, "God really saved the day when I revealed my revelation to the Pastor!"

True men and women of God do not need to sell themselves or boast to get a position. As we said in the previous chapter, *Paul was not a boaster; his fruit spoke for itself.* The Scorpion, on the other hand, will make sure that it gets the credit for anything good that happens. "Oh Pastor, if I didn't pray for that situation, it would have never worked out. I believe God is saying for me to start a prayer meeting." (Feeling the dance yet?)

A Scorpion succeeds when a leader succumbs to his own fears and insecurities. He prevails when the leader is more concerned about being approved and accepted by people rather than by God. Leaders, a Scorpion will use ***ego*** to seduce you. It will capitalize on your insecurities and then cause you to either succumb, or react egotistically. Compensating for your fears and insecurities through carnality will only end badly for you.

Regarding insecurities, this is the courtship dance at its best: The Scorpion locks its claws with its mate's and then starts the long, seductive dance. It goes up and down, backward and forward, to the right and to the left. With each moment the male/victim is getting more and more excited, but it is up to the female/perpetrator to say when. It is the same with the Scorpion-influenced person. It locks its claws on your shortcomings and pretends to soothe them. So you keep confiding more and more, but approval never really seems to come. They say things like, "I had to leave the other church because the pastor was off in left field." This is when you are entering into an unholy relationship. It may not seem like it, but it is. This is when fear says, "As long as Sister Saystoomuch stays at my church, I know I'm not off-base." Yet, when approval finally does come, it's certain death. *You're stung!* If you listen to the Scorpion's words of flattery, you will listen to its words of bitterness!

Allow your security in God to develop instead of your ego! There are only three aspects of godly approval that you need to be concerned with:

1. Know you are called of God.

2. Meet the scriptural qualifications for ministry.

3. Elders in the Body of Christ, who are approved of God, recognize your call and affirmed you into the ministry.

If your approval is going to come from Sister Irma Fullofaspirit or Brother Clay Controlyourlife, the Scorpion has got you in an incestuous mating dance. Incestuous and perverse, because they should be the sheep you are feeding, but instead you are treating them like graced elders. You begin to believe that you and the church cannot live without this person's spiritual input. (Guess what? **If your church was born of God, it will survive without them.** Watch it; you are entering into an unholy relationship.) Instead of pastoring this person and instructing them, you begin to listen, in subtle fear of their tales. This little deceived sheep, infected by a bitter Scorpion (like an alien creature eating its way out its host), is going to enter into a relationship with you and try to be your "personal spiritual advisor." He may even want to meet with you for secret or private prayer.

Be very leery of private prayer with overly spiritual people. Many times there is another agenda on their minds and it isn't the welfare of the church. If a leader has surrendered to such a prayer meeting, the Scorpion (who is a "self-proclaimed prophet or intercessor"), will often get revelations about your life and begin to advise you, or worse, *tell others.* Because the revelations are very close to the truth, it can be intimidating. (By this time, you've already naively revealed your fears to them, so many of these revelations are nothing more than spiritually amplified information you've already provided.) Above all, remember that in the darkness there's a deceiver, only telling you enough to strike fear in your heart and fasten its claws on you.

The Bible tells that in the incestuous relationship between Lot and his daughters, they first got him drunk. As a result, he didn't even know what happened until it was too late. The Scorpion will play on your fears until you are drunk with them. Then the moment of copulation will begin. It will open to you an irresistible *supposed* word from God a *sure* solution to your challenges. Once the temptation begins, you want to go back for more. Remember the female scorpion? When the male didn't get away in time, instead of just copulating, she devoured him as an after-romance snack. In the same way, you become intoxicated with the doubt of your own abilities in God. Then the spiritual incest takes place. You tell them of your marital struggles, financial troubles, concerns about church growth and so on. Finally, you are nothing more than a dry husk. This demon has been sucking the spiritual life out of you, day after day. Drunk with anxiety, you have submitted to the Scorpion and become embittered with the congregation. You may lash out from the pulpit with bitter words, thus wounding the sheep and losing them, little by little.

Pastors, stay away from "spiritual advisors" who through their actions imply that you're spiritually impotent and extract spiritual life from you. Every pastor should have colleagues and mentors who advise them, but not of this sort! In the Bible, such unacceptable advisors are called mediums, witches, and diviners. When King Saul went to the witch of Endor for advisement, he found himself in big trouble!

Finally, if the mission of the Scorpion is successful, the leader or pastor can fall morally as well, most likely into sexual sin (especially if the advisor is of the opposite sex). Equally dreadful, the leader will leave the ministry with deep discouragement.

I mentioned sexual sin because of the nature of the spirit involved. It is incestuous, which is ultimately by definition a sexual act. *The leader, who's been looking for resolve to his fears and perceived spiritual impotency (by sources other than God), will eventually find it in sensual pleasures.* Such resolve comes with statements like, "I couldn't even tell my wife my problems. She didn't understand what I was going through. But Thelma Theadvisor did, so I just couldn't help myself. I felt comfort. Before I knew it, we were in bed." This is not only a lie, but the fruit of self-deception. There is a whole process that one goes through before committing such deeds. The concern is trying to resolve spiritual issues through carnal means.

As far as discouragement, consider that this demon has been steadily working, chipping away bit by bit. The leader of God has doubted himself little by little, until finally no spiritual potency is left. Any faith in God or the call on his life has been transformed into trusting this incestuous relationship. He may even doubt his own salvation! One pastor told me (after being bitten by this evil spirit and pastoring several churches without addressing the poison in his inner life), that he wasn't even sure if he had a relationship with God. Can you imagine? Can you conceive of a pastor preaching weekly to a congregation who is drinking from his spiritual well, while he's not even sure if he has a relationship with God? This really happened!

At the very least, the Scorpion will betray the pastor to the elders. The Scorpion will inform the leadership of the ministerial or personal problems the pastor is having, usually making the problems sound worse than they are. In many cases the elders already knew of the issues, but the Scorpion makes them sound way out of proportion. The poison is focused on creating doubt about the pastor's abilities in the minds of leadership. If they receive this poisonous drink, they will always have problems trusting their pastor. Instead of covering and encouraging him, they will become critical. If they are not careful, they will become Scorpions themselves.

If the Scorpion is of the opposite sex and really got a hold of its victim, the leadership may get a call that sounds something like this, "I can't live with myself. I think the pastor has been making passes at me and I'm feeling so tempted." Before you know it, this devil is *seeding* the leadership and has them subconsciously looking for these problems in their pastor. To add to the conflict, the pastor has less resistance for fighting the problems the Scorpion is creating. The pastor has been stung and is being pulled apart piece by piece. The devil is scourging his life away. In the end, the elders are looking at the pastor with distrust and will eventually confront him with his resignation papers.

> *"But beware of men, for they will deliver you up to councils and scourge you in their synagogues." (Matthew 10:17/NKJV)*

> *"Still others had trial of mockings and scourgings, yes, and of chains and imprisonment." (Hebrews 11:36/NKJV)*

Pastor, ask God to send you people who are willing to love God's work and love you. Ask God to give you the discernment to know who really loves the Lord *and* His work. Remember always to be real and transparent with your leadership and the sheep. But at the same time, do not burden the sheep with heavy situations that will not bless them. Keep those things for the elders that are working side by side with you. If you feel you cannot trust your leadership, either you need some new trustworthy leaders or you need personal ministry for insecurity. The other issue could also be that you may have an inappropriate need to be in control (which more than likely comes from a root of insecurity). Be careful that you do not substitute your needed Divine confidence with arrogance and pride. If you don't get the personal ministry you need, the Scorpion will take what it needs to survive ... you or the sheep. *Or both!*

CHAPTER 4

SCORPION PASS: A CULTURAL ISSUE

We have examined the poisoning of the innocent, the bitter betrayal of insurrection, and attempts to destroy God's leaders. We also dissected this villain and exposed its modes of operation. With this information, you know that the only way to escape Scorpion Pass or to prevent one from occurring is through the anointing and authority of God. Jesus said that He has given us authority to trample on the Scorpion (Luke 10:18-20). Yet the secret to that authority is focusing on the fact that our names are written in Heaven. This is more than just a roll call; it implies that we are members of God's Kingdom under His authority and of His spiritual quality (nature). The fact that Satan must heed our command is because we are in line (of the same quality), as God's authority.

As we have learned, many times we trample on the Scorpion after we find one. But by the time we find an active Scorpion, it is usually at the apex of the situation, after it has gained some strength. To best conquer this enemy, the Apostle Paul in so many words said, *give no place to it!* So rather than looking for Scorpions in our churches (thus creating paranoia and needless witch hunts) we should focus on building a church or ministry that tramples such evil as it marches forward accomplishing the Kingdom's purpose. (The definition and discussion of such purpose and spiritual quality will be in Chapter 6.)

In our current culture in the western world, almost any person that truly surrenders to the Lordship of Christ has already set himself against insurrective temptation. Looking at life in the west, particularly in America since the early 1950s, it's been common practice to rebel against government, oppress the weak, and mock authority. Just look at almost any late-night talk show. The content of the opening monologue embraces the mocking of our leaders, laughing at the unfortunate, and saying whatever makes you feel better, even if it means degrading another person.

It's a repulsive thought to a mature Christian, to mock Christ's authority, to laugh at the unfortunate and to simply say whatever makes you feel good, especially if it hurts another. Yet, even though we, as believers, would not admit to such crimes, many times we commit the crime and don't even recognize it. This is why the spirit of the Scorpion has had such success in ministries and we find ourselves almost powerless to defeat it.

We have been raised in a world where darkness has housed creatures (both human and spiritual) that oppress, manipulate, and seduce. As a result, we are afraid of being abused by authority, being part of a "group" unless it meets our emotional needs, and so on. We also resist following leadership unless he or she fits a multitude of emotional criteria that is almost impossible to attain. Because of this, pastoring or leading a ministry in the western world has been reduced to a profession, rather than a high calling from the Eternal Lord of Light.

Even then, few professions carry the expectations as that of pastor. If we go to a doctor, we would have to wait our turn until he could see us and have our payment ready in advance. If he told us we needed to quit smoking because our lives depended upon it, we would throw away our cigarettes in fear and then (being good Christians) join a cause like Americans Against Second Hand Smoke. But when it comes to the minister, if he doesn't see us when we want, we let him know how he failed us. We expect to get the best quality biblical counsel available as long as it agrees with what we want to hear. If the minister brings us into accountability and tells us we need to quit practicing a detrimental behavior, we scrutinize what he said and vote against raising his housing allowance at the next board meeting. We simply take the baggage that Satan bred in us about authority and join the church.

This brings us to another perspective we need to make mention of: You don't join a church, you become a life-giving aspect of its reality. When you come to Christ, you become a part of His family and a member of His Kingdom. For many of us, when the man or woman of God speaks in authority, we look at them as if they insulted us in a foreign language, "What in the world did you say? Who do you think you are? You're just a pastor!"

While we understand the theology of Christianity, and even desire to live as Christ did, we still have to realize that God governs His Kingdom, *His way.* It's in this area of government and its function that we are in a different country, or better said, *under rule of a different system.* It isn't that we directly refuse to be submitted to God's way; it's the idea of respecting authority that troubles us. It's not that we mind the idea of submitting to God. **It's those imperfect humans that He has put in authority over us. That's where the problem lies!**

We come from a world that says, "Run your own course... If it feels good, do it... Plan your own destiny..." Then we come to Christ and we say things like, "I'm submitted to Jesus and will do whatever He tells me. Christ is my Lord. So Pastor, understand I know what's best for me. I am under the authority of the Spirit and the Word, so I will handle this as I see fit." Ugh! The ego, the source of all darkness, is a crafty, wicked thing. It is integrated into our very being. Its spiritual quality is one and the same with Satan himself. The scriptures says:

"The heart is deceitful above all things, And desperately wicked; Who can know it?"
(Jeremiah 17:9/NKJV)

If we were to really consider what it means to be an aspect of Christ, we would never conceive of such behavior. Yet if we say that we are submitted to the Word and Spirit, let's start by surrendering to the scripture in this area.

"Obey your spiritual leaders, and do what they say. Their work is to watch over your souls, and they are accountable to God. Give them reason to do this with joy and not with sorrow. That would certainly not be for your benefit." (Hebrews 13:17/NLT)

I remember some years ago, I dealt with a young man who had difficulty with the way I addressed an issue as it related to those he was working with in the church. My approach offended him. This took me back for a moment. I went to the Lord asking if I had a problem, and in one sense I did. I realized that I had assumed things about my pastoral relationship to him that he never understood or accepted. In addition, even though we spent time together, fellowshipped and so on, he did not understand what was happening. It was to the point where the clearer (and more redundant) I became, the more offended he became. In the end, he wanted to leave the church, yet he told me that "God spoke to his heart" to stay. He also told me that he needed to talk with me, although *not as his pastor,* but as his friend. When I inquired of him about what, he said it was regarding me, this situation and in some way, the church. While this sounds innocent and sincere, we must realize that God has a divine order that we should not violate. Asking me to remove myself from being his pastor so he could talk with me as a "friend" would have opened a spiritual door of disorder akin to Pandora's Box. It would be like a son who was just disciplined by his father, requesting his father to not be a father for a minute, but his friend, so he could talk with him about the situation. One thing our children don't need (be they natural *or spiritual)*, is another friend whose advice they can do with as they please. What our children strongly need is parents who love them enough to allow open communication, but also to discipline and not compromise themselves.

Keep in mind our culture! How many times have you seen a television situation comedy in which the father is a nice guy, but makes stupid decisions until the children teach him a lesson? Now, before we blame too much television as the problem, let's also remember that it depicts a lot of images people already have in their minds. It's a vicious circle. Art (through whatever medium) depicts the mind and status of a culture, and the culture shapes the art. It is cyclical; the more the culture feeds on it, the more the culture affirms itself.

In the mind of God, art is intended not only to depict the current status, but His prophetic intention. The various arts are a vehicle the Holy Spirit uses to express the lessons of the past, the situations of the present and the Divine intent of the future.

Without truly gifted, healthy, non-religious believers at the hand of media, the arts fall prey to whatever image "the void" produces. People come into the Kingdom in the same way. They come with their own image of what they believe the Kingdom and its government is like. Thus, when something doesn't go right, they just tell the pastor or leader how they want him to deal with the situation. If he doesn't heed their demands, they hold the threat of finances or attendance over his head. In truth, this is juvenile, much like a teenager who sees his growing need for responsibility as life being unfair.

Relating to God and to those in his Kingdom is something God takes very seriously. We have recited many, many times in the Lord's model prayer, *"Thy Kingdom come. Thy will be done in earth, as it is in Heaven."* It's one thing to pray it; it's another thing to live it! If we really want God's Kingdom to manifest in our lives, then we must understand how He does things. If we want His will done in earth in the same manner it is done in Heaven, we will have to renew our thinking about what that means. Keep in mind that Lucifer (the first fellow who thought about insurrection) did not last very long in God's presence.

Understand that many churches and sects of Christianity have different ways of administrating government. There are administrations where the congregation elects the pastor, elders, and deacons. In others, pastors are appointed by bishops or superintendents. Some have boards or trustees. But regardless of the type of administration, the anointing for government is the same. To truly see God's power and love manifested to the world, we must learn to respect His authority and His anointed *by His standards.*

A good example of this is in the Old Testament between young David and King Saul. In this case, even after Saul spent so much energy trying to slay David, David still had great respect for God's divine order and God's anointed. It's also interesting to note how many times in the Old and New Testament, that the "Kingdom of God" is typified by the "kingdom of David." In spite of David's many faults and failings (and they were drastic, including adultery and murder), God still considered him *a man after His heart.* One of the reasons for being called such a man and having this reputation in God's Kingdom was David's keen attention to respecting the anointed. The Bible says that at the end of King Saul's life, he was in the midst of being overtaken by his enemies and requested that a young stranger help him commit suicide (See 1 Samuel 31, and 2 Samuel 1). When the young stranger came to David and told him the story, David was furious and had him struck dead.

> *"David asked him, 'Why were you not afraid to lift your hand to destroy the Lord's anointed?' Then David called one of his men and said, 'Go, strike him down!' So he struck him down, and he died. For David had said to him, 'Your blood be on your own head. Your own mouth testified against you when you said, 'I killed the Lord's anointed.' David took up this lament concerning Saul and his son Jonathan..." (2 Samuel 1:14-17/NIV)*

We, the people of God, would rarely say we have committed the crime of dishonoring authority, but we have. We've done it through ignorance or simple disrespect. These ingredients are the foretaste of insurrection and a prelude to opening the Kingdom gate to the Scorpion.

On the other hand, **we, in authority, cannot abuse this privilege.** We cannot hide our sins and failings behind the scripture that the people are not to touch His anointed. Many times, the anointed have tried to conceal their sinfulness and inappropriate behavior by such scripture. While God is gracious in saying such, we must never forget as God's leaders we are tending HIS SHEEP, NOT OUR OWN! While God protects His leaders from false accusations and repentant failings, He is also very jealous of His Sheep and those that deal inappropriately with them (Jeremiah 23:1; Ezekiel 34:2).

Because each of us have the Spirit and the Word of God, we should be able to respect God's leaders (as imperfect as they may sometimes be) and know that following those who follow Christ is not a little thing with God. In the case of David and King Saul, Saul was not even following the Lord, but his own fears and insecurities. But David still had great respect for his position.

When that young man I mentioned earlier asked me to speak with him, (not as his pastor, but as a friend) I went to the Lord and asked for counsel. I also spoke to our eldership, and to my pastoral mentor. The unanimous response was that it would not be a good idea. I told the young man I would not speak with him in that manner. I explained what God placed on my heart and what I received from Godly counsel. I exhorted him to obey what God had told him, which was to be a part of the church. I told him to give any issues to God and go on building His Kingdom. He told me he would stay, but would have a hard time submitting to the church eldership because of this issue. I explained to him that the same God who told him to stay at the church, also said (in the Bible) to submit and respect church authority. (I also suggested that God knew His own scripture when He told him to stay.) He agreed, yet after a few weeks and several interactions, he and his family left the church. I was sorry to see him go. He said he was sorry too, but he felt he needed to leave. Clearly he did not have an understanding of God's authority in the local church.

> *"If someone says, 'I love God,' and hates his brother, he is a liar; for he who does not love his brother whom he has seen, how can he love God whom he has not seen? And this commandment we have from Him: that he who loves God must love his brother also."*
>
> *(1 John 4:20-21/NKJV)*

If you know that God has engrafted you into a local church *(and every Christian should be engrafted in a church according to the scripture),* the next step is to ask the Holy Spirit for direction on how to best be in relationship and follow its leadership. Keep in mind that leaders will make mistakes and we should not crucify them when they do. After all, church members expect to be forgiven for mistakes and continue to grow when they fall; let's extend the same love for our leaders when they stumble.

NOTE: This does not mean we excuse inappropriate behavior, sin, or immoral conduct in leadership. But let us lovingly hold them accountable and properly restore them if necessary.

You may think, "I didn't say a word when I got hurt by them. But I'm fine now. I just don't see eye to eye with the leadership anymore." That could be the problem. Maybe you never said an evil word, but in your heart you've been unable to release and forgive them. Maybe because of your upbringing or life experience, you would have never seen eye to eye *because of their position* anyway. Thus, you are not able to walk in a proper relationship with them, but you call it a difference of opinion. I've heard people say, "Well, after *they* realize what *they* did, then I'll forgive them." Unfortunately, that's not the way the Kingdom of God works. **Your unforgiveness is not *their* problem; *it's yours.*** Just because leaders make mistakes doesn't mean they cease being your leaders. Many parents make mistakes with their children, but they are still their parents. The same is true for pastors.

We, in the church, deal with God and His leaders a lot like teenagers deal with their parents. They want them to provide nourishment and shelter, but never make a mistake. I've counseled parents of teenagers who in their frustration made themselves slaves of their children. When they want money, the parents give them money. When they want to go somewhere, the parents change their schedule to give them a ride. When they don't want to do their chores, mom and dad do it. Why? So Johnny or Sheryl won't get upset and make life miserable. Sound familiar? As most parents know, it's not that they want to keep their teenager from having fun with friends or that they mind rearranging their schedules to accommodate their needs, **it simply comes down to a need for respect and fulfillment of responsibility.**

One of the reasons parents have a problem with receiving respect and seeing their children be responsible, is that they, themselves, have the same problem with God's anointed. They want the man or woman of God to give them the best spiritual food, clean the church, make sure the bus ministry picks them up when they need a ride, sacrifice financially if necessary, and take whatever little casual respect is offered. *One of the greatest things a leader can ever receive is respect and the fulfillment of a member's responsibility.*

As in the case with David and Saul, authority is not just a position a pastor or leader holds, but a position that has been delegated by God. A while ago, I was reading in the book of Matthew about the man with the palsy, who was brought to Jesus by his friends. The Bible said:

"So He got into a boat, crossed over, and came to His own city. Then behold, they brought to Him a paralytic lying on a bed. When Jesus saw their faith, He said to the paralytic, 'Son, be of good cheer; your sins are forgiven you.'" (Matthew 9:1-2/NKJV)

I remember at that moment I prayed, "Lord, I don't want the kind of faith that others affirm, or faith that I think I have; I WANT THE FAITH THAT YOU

CAN SEE!" In almost a flash, I felt the tugging of the Holy Spirit to read the chapter before, about the centurion and his paralytic servant.

> *"Now when Jesus had entered Capernaum, a centurion came to Him, pleading with Him, saying, 'Lord, my servant is lying at home paralyzed, dreadfully tormented.' And Jesus said to him, 'I will come and heal him.' The centurion answered and said, 'Lord, I am not worthy that You should come under my roof. But only speak a word, and my servant will be healed. For I also am a man under authority, having soldiers under me. And I say to this one, Go, and he goes; and to another, Come, and he comes; and to my servant, Do this, and he does it.' When Jesus heard it, He marveled, and said to those who followed, 'Assuredly, I say to you, I have not found such great faith, not even in Israel!'" (Matthew 8:5-11/NKJV)*

I was struck once again by this issue of how we understand authority. Jesus said to the centurion, *"...I have not found so great faith..."* This was the answer to my prayer, but again it was directly connected to how I perceive authority. Jesus *saw great faith* because the centurion **saw His authority.** We can learn much from this scripture. The centurion stated that he was in authority because it was given to him. This is a great key. The Holy Spirit then spoke to my heart and said, **"The measure of your faith that I can see is based on the measure of My authority in your life that you can see."**

The centurion saw that Jesus exercised authority in healing because He was under the Father's authority. In contrast, as we look back to our comment about David and Saul, when the young man helped Saul commit suicide, he was not just helping a lost king bring his woes to an end; he was destroying God's divine order. He was taking a man out of position whom God had ordained for that position.

Brothers and sisters in Christ, please consider this. If God anoints and appoints His leaders, He can also remove and judge those same leaders. We, as the people of God, need first to be submitted to God's Word and the Holy Spirit in order to properly follow His anointed. The centurion understood that he was a soldier and had authority because it was given to him by one of greater authority. In the same manner, he understood that those who were under him, in submission, were expected to follow out of that regard. To disrespect him was to disrespect the one who gave him his authority. This is why he had great faith. He knew Jesus had authority, because a "Greater One" gave Him that authority. He also knew that all Jesus needed to do was speak the Word, and that which was under His authority had to obey. When it comes to church leaders, the Apostle Paul put it this way:

"Not that we have dominion over your faith, but are fellow workers for your joy; for by faith you stand." (2 Corinthians 1:24/NKJV)

God did not give authority to leaders so they could rule over people just to satisfy their own lust or ego, although we must admit such has happened. Ideally, God put leadership in our churches (See Ephesians 4, and 1 Corinthians 12) not only so we can hear messages about blessing and have free counseling, but to establish His vision for our communities and mature His people. Some of the key reasons the spirit of the Scorpion breeds in our congregations is disrespect, a causal attitude, and a lack of knowledge of Kingdom authority.

CHAPTER 5

WAR IN THE DESERT

One of the best and most concise lessons of understanding Kingdom authority appears in the book of Exodus. First, we find the people upset and angry with Pastor Moses and his associate, Aaron. Here we clearly see what God thinks about quarreling with His anointed.

> *"Therefore the people contended with Moses, and said, 'Give us water, that we may drink.' So Moses said to them, 'Why do you contend with me? Why do you tempt the Lord?'" (Exodus 17:2/NKJV)*

The Hebrew word used for "contend" in the verse is יָרֶב (yahrev; in the imperfect tense) and can be translated "to chide or argue." But what is more telling about this word is that its family root is רב (rav) which means "teacher or master." It is from this word we get the word *rabbi,* which in Hebrew actually means "my teacher." In this case, the idea of using this word to describe contention is more than just dealing with conflict. It is dealing with one forming the argument as a master or teacher himself. If it was just an issue of having a difference of opinion, an argument and a strong discussion, the Hebrew verb that could have been used is וִכָּח (vikakh). But יָרֶב is used to reveal that the ones speaking against Moses were trying to make themselves his equal in stature and position.

This changes the playing field of what is going on. This is not an honest difference of opinion; this is about the hearts of those arguing. The scripture places such attitudes on the same level as *tempting God.* Someone may say, "But what if the pastor is wrong? What if he or the elders make a mistake?" Then BELIEVE GOD and treat them the way you would want to be treated if you made the mistake!

If you're a board member and you're going to hire a pastor, keep this in mind; you have been given the holy task of recognizing the anointing on a man or woman's life. But once the hiring is done, you must be willing to follow and be submitted to God's anointed. You are not their HR department; you are their support. In addition, it's your responsibility to make sure they receive the respect and financial blessing they are worthy of, according to scripture.

> *"The elders who rule well are to be considered worthy of double honor, especially those who work hard at preaching and teaching." (1 Timothy 5:17/NASU)*

You may wonder, "What shall I look for in a pastor?"

First, does he or she understand the relationship of God's authority and the humility required to walk in it? This is VERY important! We don't need super-preachers who put themselves in the position of a demigod.

Second, is he or she submitted to authority? Does he have a pastor or spiritual mentor who is seasoned in Godly character and can offer Godly counsel?

Third, does he or she recognize the moving of God's Spirit in individuals within the church?

Now you may think, "How in the world do I determine that he or she has all these traits with just a resume, a couple of interviews and a few Sunday sermons?" Now you understand the weight of the honor you have in making such a selection. Thus, rather than scrutinize, *recognize* God in the imperfect vessel and stand by him or her.

It all comes down to this final example in Exodus. It depends on our willingness to trust God with our lives when He leads us to a local church.

> *"Now Amalek came and fought with Israel in Rephidim. And Moses said to Joshua, "Choose us some men and go out, fight with Amalek. Tomorrow I will stand on the top of the hill with the rod of God in my hand." So Joshua did as Moses said to him, and fought with Amalek. And Moses, Aaron, and Hur went up to the top of the hill. And so it was, when Moses held up his hand, that Israel prevailed;*

and when he let down his hand, Amalek prevailed. But Moses' hands became heavy; so they took a stone and put it under him, and he sat on it. And Aaron and Hur supported his hands, one on one side, and the other on the other side; and his hands were steady until the going down of the sun. So Joshua defeated Amalek and his people with the edge of the sword. Then the Lord said to Moses, "Write this for a memorial in the book and recount it in the hearing of Joshua, that I will utterly blot out the remembrance of Amalek from under heaven." And Moses built an altar and called its name, The-Lord-Is-My-Banner; for he said, "Because the Lord has sworn: the Lord will have war with Amalek from generation to generation." (Exodus 17:6-16/NKJV)

Can you imagine the great victory? From this event another revelation of God is opened to us: נִסִּי יְהוָה "Yahweh Nissy", which literally means, "Yahweh I continually hold." Another way of putting it is, "Yahweh our Standard!" These scriptures show us the sure victory. They show us how to win our cities to Christ, heal the brokenhearted, cast out devils, conquer sin, and enjoy the promised victory.

The scripture begins with Moses giving a command to Joshua to take some men from the congregation and go to battle. Note that Joshua did not say, "Well, okay Moses, but first let me go pray about it and see if that's what God wants for me." He already knew what God wanted from him; *he knew it was to be a part of God's tribe and follow God's anointed.*

Many people "have to pray" about what leadership says regarding their part in the local church because they have not already prayed about their connectivity to the church. Let me put it another way. If I, as a pastor, ask you to be an usher, there is nothing wrong with saying, "Thank you pastor, but I never considered that before; may I pray about this and see what God says in my heart?" On the other hand, once you become an usher, if every time I ask you to help in some ushering capacity you still have to pray about it, then we have real a problem. You may be thinking, "Duhh! I understand that!" Yet countless times, when it comes to raising money for the building fund, attending Bible study, being committed to the prayer group (non-Scorpion ones, of course), we start to over-spiritualize to accommodate our egos.

I know of people who have attended church for over a decade who are still praying about whether or not they should tithe. Can you imagine? When I became a husband and a father, it became my responsibility to provide for my family. Therefore I don't need to pray about whether or not I should provide for my family when I become discouraged because of problems on the job. I may need to pray for another job, but not about my connection to my family or my responsibly.

Accordingly, Joshua went and gathered the men together. This is the next point: *the men of the congregation were committed to those in authority, and to each other.* They did not say to Joshua,

"Maybe we need to get the committee together to vote on this." Neither did they say, "If Moses wants me to fight for this cause, let him get out of his comfortable little tent (office) and tell me himself!" No! They did not say anything. Instead, they got their swords and went to battle!

In the same breath Moses spoke to Joshua, he also explained to him that he, Moses, was going to stand on the top of the hill and hold the staff in his hand. In other words, "I am going to stand in faith by the authority God has given me for your success." This is exactly what Paul said to us in the scripture we read earlier, *"It is not that we have dominion over your faith, but are helpers of your joy..."* I don't know about you, but if I was going to go battle, it would give me tremendous joy to know that my pastor was standing in faith for my success.

The next important part of these scriptures is found in verse 11. When Moses' staff (the symbol of God's authority) was held up high, Israel would obtain a winning advantage. When his hand sank down, the enemy would gain the advantage. This tells us the importance of **holding God's anointed authority in high esteem and respect.** It also shows us that Moses, the man, could not hold up such authority on his own. ***He, in his own frailty, needed help.*** Enter the elders and ministry leadership. Rather than standing around judging Moses' inability to uphold authority and saying, "Hey Moses, you're slipping and we can't have that. Keep dropping that staff and we'll have to discuss whether you still have a job." Instead of scrutinizing Moses' human weakness and tiredness, they took a stone and put it under him. Thus, they made his stand of faith as secure as possible so he could hold the rod of authority as long as possible. They did not say, "We want you to be comfortable pastor, so we'll hold the rod for awhile. You go and find yourself a rock to sit on." No! They kept the authority where it belonged and they went and got the rock.

Men and women of God, you do not need to take charge of the leader's position when he gets weary. That is also out of divine order unless he delegates the task to you (See Exodus 24:14).

Years ago, a "former preacher" came to our church and told me that God called him to help me in the ministry. That translated into, "Pastor, let me preach every few weeks and you take a rest." The one (and only) time I let him preach was when I was a guest speaker at another church. Toward the end of the message he said to the congregation, "I know Pastor said only to preach for so many minutes, but he won't mind if I go over." From what I was told, he wasn't saying much to begin with, just shouting and jerking, and not only did I mind that he did not heed my instruction, but the people minded as well. This was not a help to me or the congregation, but a nuisance. If you are an elder, deacon, board member or trustee, keep in mind that *helping is assisting your leader do his job the best way possible.* Can you imagine Moses trying to hold his staff up and wandering around looking for a rock at the same time? Can you imagine him trying to hold the staff up and trying to maneuver the rather large rock into position? What would Joshua have thought in the heat of the battle, as he looked up to Moses and found him walking around searching for something to sit on? Or worse, what if Joshua looked up for Moses and found him in the middle of a meeting with "the committee" to decide whose ministry it was to obtain the rock? Or worse even yet! Can you imagine them huddled together voting on whether or not they wanted Moses to be their pastor because he got weary holding the staff? I know what I would be thinking, "Hey you dense Pharisees! Without Moses holding up the staff we're all dead men. Do something and help our shepherd!" Thank God, that was not the case with Aaron and Hur!

After they sat Moses on the rock, they supported him and held up his arms. By them doing this, Moses was able to hold the staff as long as necessary to win the battle. By the leadership taking their position and strengthening God's anointed, the battle was won. One may say, "How will I know where my pastor needs help?" The simplest way I can answer that is, ASK! Then, when he tells you what is needed, do all you can to strengthen and empower him *by doing what needs to be done!* The scripture says that Joshua discomforted the enemy. Another way of putting it is that he and his men OVERCAME the enemy. The Living Bible says, "...Joshua and his troops, crushed the enemy...", that is exactly what Jesus said we are to do, CRUSH THE SCORPION!

Because Moses' authority and function was upheld, it gave joy, comfort, and victory to Joshua and his men during the battle. So let's get this image in our minds: **Moses stood in faith and authority while Aaron and Hur upheld him in his position.**

On the other hand, we need to be educated about the flow of authority and respect the ministry function of another. What do you think this scenario would look like to a man on the battlefield who does not understand God's flow of authority? Well for one, he would probably be in the heat of the battle, glance up the hill and see the picture of Aaron and Hur upholding Moses arms as he sat on the rock. The uneducated would probably get upset, stop fighting and get a few guys to listen to his complaint. "Look at Pastor Moses! We're fighting down here like mad dogs and he and the other big shots are sitting around holding a stick in the air! If he's such a great man of faith and power, why isn't he down here fighting like the rest of us?" The man could get so angry that he would turn his bow and arrow (which was meant for the enemy), and shoot at Moses. The Bible says:

> *"Their tongue is an arrow shot out; It speaks deceit; One speaks peaceably to his neighbor with his mouth, But in his heart he lies in wait." (Jeremiah 9:8/NKJV)*

By the arrow of his mouth, this warrior would take himself right out of the divine flow and shoot Moses. Most likely, this is not a true Scorpion; rather, a zealous new member who does not understand Godly authority. But just because he doesn't understand, doesn't mean he is exempt from the consequences of his actions.

Continuing with our hypothetical story, Moses is struck deep in the heart. He falls back on his elders and his arm sinks to the ground. His hand opens as he is paralyzed by the pain and *the rod* falls to the ground and rolls down the hill. Can you imagine the army watching this? Can you imagine them seeing "that stick" roll down the hill? "Yikes! We all just became Amalekite food!" It would mean the annihilation of God's people by the enemy. The Bible said that if Moses' hand sank, the enemy would win the battle. Can you imagine if *the rod of God's anointed authority* really fell to the ground and rolled down the hill? (I don't want to think about it.) Chances are the Torah would end right there with no New Testament to follow!

Respect for God's anointed and honoring His ordained authority is the key to faith and victory in the life of every believer. *There are no exceptions.* One cannot help realize this when we take a look at all the Biblical titles we use to relate to God: Father, Lord, King, Prince, Master, Alpha and Omega, Captain, Messiah, Counselor and so on. There are more, but this should give us a clue that authority and successful Christian living (not to mention victory over evil), are like *wet* and *water;* you cannot have one without the other!

I'm sure there are questions about those leaders who fall into sin and how we are to deal with them, while still being submitted. There are several answers, some quite complex (as explained in my book "Why Ministers Fall"), but the shortest explanation is found in whether or not the leader himself is connected to healthy relationships and authority. If he is, usually such mistakes are avoided or minimized. Thus, when leaders are in such relationships, all we need to focus on is prayer for their success, rather than their potential for failure. Also, let's remind ourselves that most pastors and leaders enter the ministry with a call from God and a heart for His people. They rarely set out to fall or be hurtful. As a matter of fact, we, the people of God, can help minimize some of the temptations that can lead to a minister's fall. If we take the attitude of Aaron, Hur, and Joshua, we can help cut down the pressures that aid in the failure of God's anointed and encourage them to greater success. In turn, this also means greater success for us.

Before we continue, we need to reflect on Moses and the children of Israel. Moses never made it into the Promised Land, but this was not God's intention. Moses sabotaged his own success by disobeying God in the desert of Zin, but did you ever wonder why? Did it ever occur to us, as believers, the children of God, the members of a local church and fellow laborers in the ministry, that if the children of Israel would have been respectful and submitted, Moses would not have been put in a position to fall (Psalms 106:32)?

It's possible that Moses still wouldn't have finished the journey into the Promised Land (which is just speculation), but it sure would have been a lot easier if the people were submitted, respectful, and forgiving. Maybe before our church finds itself in such unnecessary challenges, we should crush the Scorpion before it ever sets its appendages in the door! We could start by repenting of our attitudes toward God's anointed. We could continue by purposing in our hearts to fight the enemy and not our leaders. We can assure victory by training newcomers to treat authority properly through our conduct and Godly actions. Please take a moment right now, prayerfully bow your head and let God deal with your heart.

"Dear Lord Jesus, Head of the Church, forgive me for the many times I did not offer respect to the people you anointed to lead within Your Church. Lord, cleanse me for the times my pride spoke against Your leaders and for the times I entertained condemning thoughts without knowing all the details of a situation. Forgive me and purge me of self-centeredness and self-righteousness. I clearly understand that You are the reason any of us enter Your Kingdom. Lord Jesus, I put my faith in You, acknowledging that the Body of Christ is Your Church and that You can handle any situation. I humbly submit to You, Your Word and Your Spirit and will do all I can to build God's Kingdom. I commit to pray for my pastor and his family, the church ministry leaders, and my fellow believers with whom I serve. I commit to stand firmly in an attitude of humility, compassion, patience, and self-control with all my brothers and sisters in Christ. In Jesus name I pray. Amen."

People of God, fall in love with God's anointed and treasure the gift of your leaders. Don't admire them as some television celebrity, but as a fellow laborer in

God's Kingdom. They are sent to you from God. Treat them with the highest honor and respect. Esteem your pastor. By doing so, you uphold an aspect of the authority of God in your life.

CHAPTER 6

THE STING IN THE WHIRLWIND INTERCESSION AND THE PROPHETIC

Over the last 20 years or so, there's been a great movement in the local church toward intercession, the prophetic, and the ministry of the prophet. Because of where God desires to take His Church, it became necessary to raise up strong intercessory prayer teams, as well as prophetic insight to those who pray. For the same reason, a measure of clarity came to the ministry of the prophet as far as function and purpose. However, because of the needed function of these ministries, the Scorpion has seen them as a key target to accomplish his purposes.

One of the anomalies of the seemingly motionless desert is the dust storm or whirlwind. When this occurs it catches up all kinds of debris and small critters. The last thing a prayer group needs is a Scorpion to be caught up in a whirlwind and flung into the middle of the camp while the divine strategies of God are being revealed.

Since the time we started our ministry over 25 years ago, we, too, have had a great emphasis on the prophetic and prayer (even before it became popular). We saw those as important parts of the church's progression. As a senior leader traveling and ministering in the United States and overseas, I have found there is a consistency of issues with the Scorpion in these areas of ministry. I have had the privilege to teach and help establish prophetic prayer groups. I have also had the blessing of mentoring some prophets as well as other five-fold ministry gifts. But sadly, I must confess, many of the situations I have encountered were after Scorpion-like casualties occurred. I would love to tell you that I have been able to start a prophetic prayer group that has been consistent and successful with no issues, but that's not the case.

One of the highlights of our ministry some years ago was a citywide prayer group that was founded by an elder and prophet in our church. This prayer group grew with many churches participating. The group existed for 17 years (which one might claim as success in itself). Eventually its founder trained up a new leader, set them in position and the group successfully continued. Finally that leader turned the prayer group over to yet another leader. Unfortunately, after all the years of ministry to our community and leadership, the group got off into error and the Scorpion eventually made its way into the mix. We, the pastoral community, had to disband the group. It was a sad day after almost two decades of positive impact.

It is through the experience of pastoring, traveling, leading prayer groups, and overseeing the leadership of a city prayer ministry for almost two decades, that I write this chapter. One could say this is not a chapter for the fainthearted, being that we will be discussing an aspect of spirituality which is essential, but seldom addressed.

PART 1: BLACK AND WHITE
"SCORPIONS USE THEIR GIFTING
TO OBSCURE REVELATION"

*"Then the Lord answered Job **out of the whirlwind, and said:** "Who is this who darkens counsel by words without knowledge?"*
(Job 38:1-2/NKJV)

In the Hebrew language, the phrase above is:

מִן הַסְּעָרָה וַיֹּאמַר
"From the rushing windstorm, and He said..."

This is a biblical idiom for the prophetic and the appearance of the Holy Spirit to a person or group. It's important at the outset to point out that it is not a type or symbol of one's maturity or spiritual attainment that invokes the rushing windstorm to come. However, it is a representation of a prophetic place and spiritual encounter.

One of the most well-known accounts of this is in the book of Acts on the day of Pentecost.

*"And suddenly there came a sound from heaven, as of a **rushing mighty wind,** and it filled the whole house where they were sitting." (Acts 2:2/NKJV)*

Of course, this is when God released His Holy Spirit upon the Church in the Upper Room. Once again we must point out that it was not a result of any person's spiritual maturity, nor the product of some spiritual attainment in one's life. The bestowing of the Spirit and the prophetic is an act of God's mercy and grace. The idea of the whirlwind (rushing mighty wind) is actually connected to another famous encounter of the Spirit. This experience was taught in ancient times to the prophets as part of the **Divine process** in one's development of perceiving the spiritual worlds:

> *"Then I looked, and behold, **a whirlwind was coming out of the north,** a great cloud with raging fire engulfing itself; and brightness was all around it and radiating out of its midst like the color of amber, out of the midst of the fire." (Ezekiel 1:4/NKJV)*

According to the Hebrew sages, the *whirlwind* represented the first level of development where the spiritual perception and the mental faculties collide. This is not speaking of the gift of prophecy where God speaks through someone, but the development of our *perception of the spiritual worlds through our inner quality.* Consider Balaam's donkey. Beyond a doubt she spoke by the prophetic power of God, yet we cannot say that she perceived reality as a human (Numbers 22:28). This is why God warns that we should not heed the voice of soothsayers and the like; gift or function is not how we are to determine spirituality.

What you use to perceive reality determines how you see God, yourself, others, and reality. We are not just speaking of our emotional or mental state, which definitely are contributors, but we are also speaking of the raw materials, those which make up our spiritual senses. It is from those sensors, we transmit to others our spiritual state. The difference between a prophet and a soothsayer is not their gift, *but their spiritual **quality*** (Micah 3:11; 1 Timothy 5:22; Jude 10).

It is so important for us to grasp that spiritual perception and quality has no bearing on how long someone has been functioning in the gift of prophecy or how long someone has been operating in the office of prophet, or any other ministry for that matter. **The gift or the office fits into our perception and not the other way around.** Our inner spiritual quality and the transformation of our perception of reality, comes from our personal pursuit of God, not the use of His gifts. It is for this reason we must understand how God transforms our perception of reality to His. This is an essential key for the prophetic and intercessory prayer groups.

A person can be two days old since their spiritual conversion and yet prophesy profoundly (Psalms 8:2; Matthew 21:16). On the other hand, as we say in our colloquial cliché, so-and-so may have "known the Lord" for years, but that doesn't mean his inner perception and state is beyond infancy (the book of Jonah, the forth chapter, is a good example). For that matter, one of the reasons it's difficult to convince a

Scorpion to change his ways is because of "how" he sees the world around him. The fact that his gift is working or he may actually occupy a ministry office, doesn't change what he's actually transmitting in the spiritual world. **Length of time, usage of gifting, or duration in office has nothing to do with how one perceives spiritual reality or spiritual quality.** To put it plainly, if a woman blind from birth lives 30 years in that state, her perception of reality still is what it is. If she lives another five years, still without the sense of sight, just because she lived for 35 years with four senses and may have done so admirably, doesn't mean she can describe the colors of a rainbow.[MA17] **How a person perceives the world they live in, and for that matter the spiritual world around them, can determine the type of influence they bring to a group.**

The importance of discussing the matter of perception is relevant to us because, in a given prayer group or prophetic setting, different dynamics occur. In any given group you can have two mature people with the same gifting. They may have a good knowledge of scripture, live moral lives, and be able to prophesy at the drop of a hat. Yet they can also be in two very different places in their development of spiritual perception.

To fine tune our example: If a person is color blind, let's say they cannot see the primary color red. Their perception of all the colors on the color spectrum related to red will be altered. For them, red simply doesn't exist. Thus, they see the world, make decisions, and understand reality without the presence of red. It doesn't mean they see more blue or green in its place, it simply means there is a *void,* an unknown or grey. It also doesn't matter how they have progressed in maturity as a person, or how long they have been functioning in a particular manner, *the void is still there.* Their perception of reality is what it is. But if something were to change and red would be added to their color spectrum, their entire perception of reality would change.

In many cases, when people have an addition in one of the five senses, that change is mentally and emotionally dramatic. When it occurs, it may be as upsetting as if the reverse happened when they lost one of their senses. Sometimes, when a color is restored by some means, depth perception and relationships to objects change and become difficult for a season. The person may rigorously analyze and concentrate intensely on what they perceive. They fight the psychological commotion of the new, differing information. You could say they are in a *whirlwind.* Spiritually speaking, the whirlwind represents the mental/emotional *noise* a person experiences as they develop their "sense" of the spiritual world. It is very similar to gaining or restoring a physical sense.

At this stage of the Church's development in the area of the prophetic and intercession, we must expand our understanding so we don't continue making the same mistakes and keeping ourselves vulnerable to the Scorpion. On the positive side, the whirlwind represents the beginning of one's (or a group's) spiritual/prophetic perception of the higher worlds. It also represents the turbulent thoughts that get mixed into the perception as the process occurs. To make the point, even though the "download" of the gift of prophecy may have clarity, it gets mixed into the atmosphere of those through and to whom it is manifested. The atmosphere is determined by several things: the emotional, mental, and most importantly, the *perceptive quality* of a person or group. It is important to keep in mind that God usually doesn't think in terms of individuals, but in terms of the collective. When He is revealed in a group, to some measure it is because they have fulfilled His Divine prescription of two or three being gathered together in His fundamental nature, quality or form (Matthew 18:20). Thus, the turbulence is not necessarily limited to a person, but also affects the group. When the rushing mighty wind appeared in the Upper Room it did so to the entire group (literally 120 people), not just one person. Also, when the whirlwind appeared in the book of Job, not only was Job present, but his friends as well.

The scripture in Job says, "*Who is this who darkens counsel by words without knowledge?*" Another way to translate this would be:

מִי זֶה מַחְשִׁיךְ עֵצָה בְמִלִּין בְּלִי־דָעַת:
"Who's this, from which obscures counsel, speaking useless knowledge?"

Note the idea of "useless knowledge." This is not just referring to a lack of knowledge (inferring that one can learn in the future), but that the knowledge they have is *useless,* it is empty or void. To say it another way, the words they speak have a void in them, like our colorblind friend. In the case of the Scorpion, though it sounds good, their words obscure the truth from being perceived. It is like speaking about the color red, when we are blind to the color red. Hence, the Scorpion will speak in a manner that obscures the reality being said or revealed. Again to use our example; since they have no revelation of red, what they actually impart is a void. This void then veils the truth (2 Corinthians 4:2-4). This is why they seem so spiritual to some people. The victim(s) may be trying to grasp the so-called revelation, but there is no genuine revelation to be grasped! In the case of the Scorpion, not only is there a void, but the Scorpion has replaced the void with its egoistic desires, so now it obscures (darkens) any revelation that may be present within the group.

NOTE: Because a person hasn't attained some level of perception, doesn't mean that he or she is a Scorpion. They may just need to develop in their perception of the higher worlds. This is where someone who has an actual measure of perception of those spiritual worlds (not just theological knowledge), should be placed as an overseer of such a group. (We will speak more about this in Part 3 of this section.)

Scorpions look for opportunities where they can obscure the truth and vomit their egoistic utterances. One of the reasons I kept pointing out that God's voice in the whirlwind has nothing to do with maturity and longevity of position is because many Scorpions are gifted. Like Balaam's jackass, their gifts work. The issue is that their perception of reality is tainted by their inner issues and lack of defined perception, which comes from a lack in their spiritual quality. This creates a void in them first, where the only thing that fills it is the ego (the sin nature, which is contrary to Christ's). It's there we find their inflated egos having the need to speak by using their gift.

In the example of our colorblind friend, the mind fills in the void area with shades of grey where red should be. While the already existing whirlwind (the rushing mighty wind, in the good sense) is being worked through by the group to perceive what God is revealing, the Scorpion vomits its darkness like Job's friends. Once the obscurity occurs, the clarity of God's revelation is darkened and perceptive disarray comes to the group. Understand I did not say that the person, the Scorpion, creates some detailed deception; all it has to do is obscure the revelation by its utterance of *useless knowledge.* Most Scorpions are not that clever. The key for them is fulfilling their bitter, egoistic need masked by their giftedness. The group then finds themselves caught in the whirlwind (in the negative sense, *the mental noise)* and gets off focus. Once the mental noise occurs, the group is vulnerable, and the Scorpion can then sting and vomit its matter.

NOTE: It is important that prayer leaders and prophets develop their perception of the spiritual worlds so these situations can be discerned before someone in the group gets hurt. Many times these things are only noticed after conflict occurs. On the other hand, with this information a worse thing can happen if we are not developed. Because we have a member of the group underdeveloped in his perceptions, we erroneously accuse him of being a Scorpion. Such a blow to a person can infect him for life! In that case, we became the Scorpion who mistakenly accuses, yet he was never a Scorpion to begin with. As prophets and leaders, we need to attain a dimension of spiritual quality that truly opens us to spiritual reality.

PART 2: PRIMARY COLORS
"TRANSFORMING REALITY"

It is essential at this point that we understand that neither gifting, nor office, nor longevity of use, defines maturity or spiritual attainment in perception. The only way the transformation of perception occurs, is by one's inner spiritual quality matching the same spiritual quality *in Christ.* Think of it, in a reality where there is no time or distance (the spiritual world), why would my usage of a gift or office for a chronological time (physical time) matter? It doesn't! If anything, it may matter to my ego, which is the problem in the first place. The only occasion "time" matters is when I am in pursuit of Christ and *what Christ values.*

To help explain this, let's use our colorblind concept one more time. Let's say that the form, nature, and attributes of Christ are the three [MA18]primary colors: red, blue, and yellow. Then let's say in my carnal state, my attributes are black and white, therefore void of the primary colors and

119

opposite/different than Christ's. (We are not simply talking about moral sinfulness in contrast to moral rightness. Rather, we are speaking of how we perceive reality and our similarity in *quality* to Christ.) If you notice, none of my attributes match those of Christ. Thus, there is no equivalency of form. As a result, I don't perceive reality as Christ perceives it. When I come to Jesus and receive salvation, in true spiritual reality, I now, in every aspect of my being, have the same quality as Christ. However, in practical terms, I am unaware of this reality. So now I must be transformed in my inner life, develop the spiritual sensors to perceive my true spiritual quality and state (Romans 12:2; Ephesians 2:4-7). In other words, I now must discover the quality of Christ in me.

Equivalency of form is very important when it comes to spiritual perception. For me to perceive in a Christ-like manner, I must resemble and recognize His form and quality. With that in mind, *equivalency of form* can also be called, *likeness.* **In the spiritual worlds, likeness defines closeness, and closeness defines *perception.*** The one you resemble in quality is who you are close too. Knowledge and gifting have nothing to do with it. When I egoistically put an emphasis on knowledge and gifting (this is always subtle), I actually create a barrier (an obscurity) between my form and His. I actually align myself with the "god of this world" in quality and form (2 Corinthians 4:3-4).

For several years when ministering on these concepts, I have used the example of standing next to a person in the first row. I tell the congregation that just because my physical proximity is close to this person doesn't mean anything in the world of the spirit. Then, looking at a person in the last row and sitting with my hands, legs, and facial expression just like them, I say, "In the world of the spirit, because I resemble the person in the back row, I am actually closer to them through 'likeness' (equivalency of form)." **Likeness (equivalency of form), defines how I perceive reality.** *Being like Christ in the inward man means everything!* Unfortunately we have made what sins I no longer commit or my consistency as a tither, the definition of likeness. Though those things can and should be an outgrowth of what we're talking about, many times people change their outward behavior thinking they have changed their inner quality, which cannot be further from the truth! (Matthew 23:27-28; 1 Timothy 3:5) I have seen many a Scorpion become chairman of the board because they "do" the right things and "don't do" the wrong things and have a "gift"; but their inner quality is far from Christ-likeness. This is where religion, even among the most prophetic, can gain its stronghold. Yet, the more the inner quality resembles Christ, the more one can perceive reality as He perceives it. Just because my theology says, "I am like Christ" doesn't mean this has been worked out in reality. Just because one prophesies about the color blue[MA19], doesn't mean they perceive blue or walk in the quality of blue. *Irrespective of what one may say through gift or knowledge, one can only impart to others from what they have attained in their inner quality.*

Continuing with our previous example; in my current state of black and white, I may read about the three primary colors. I may hear preaching about the three primary colors. But I still have no perception of them. Consequently, I cannot live within their reality. The end product for us ministers is that we can only elevate people to the measure of form and quality we walk in. This is not bad or intended to make us feel less-than, but to encourage every minister (regardless how long they have been in ministry or the size of their ministry) to pursue Christ-likeness. Never stop! Never fall under the deception that having a large crowd, money, and impact through media, means anything regarding your spiritual quality. This may sound radical, but remember Adolph Hitler and the Rev. Jim Jones? They possessed all those things.

We can't elevate anyone to the color red regardless how many times we shout, "There is a color red," unless we actually live in the color red. This is where preaching another's revelation or teaching can become deceptive (Jeremiah 23:30). Just because we've heard and seen the fruit of what a brother or sister proclaimed, doesn't mean we can preach the same thing. If we want to benefit from that minister's revelation in the true sense, we must create meaningful relationships. Then, either we need to invite that minister to preach it to us and our congregations, or sit under his or her teaching until we have attained in quality and form what that portion (ministry) is revealing. When we don't do this, we "bring Christ down" to our level of perception, which doesn't reveal anything to us or through us (Romans 10:6; 2 Corinthians 5:16/CJB).

What this state actually does is "obscure" (darkens) the true perception and character of Christ. To make matters worse, I can deceive myself into believing I am still Christ-like. In actuality, I have redefined Christ into my image, rather than mine being transformed into His. This is the difference between dwelling in religiosity and reality. When true inner transformation occurs, my inner form is awakened to my true form in Christ. Then, as my form equals His, my perception of the spiritual worlds open to the same as Christ's in that measure.

To put it another way, if an aspect of my inner form, say that of black or white, starts to become similar to one of Christ's (the primary color of blue for example), then I can perceive that color with its gradations. Because an aspect of my inner quality has become similar in form, I can now perceive a new dimension of reality. The more my inner world of black and white is transformed into red, blue, and yellow, the more I will be able to perceive the worlds: red, blue, and yellow. Thus, when I intercede, prophesy, preach or teach, I also impart a spiritual awakening to the group in that aspect of the nature and character of Christ.

CHAPTER 7

DARKNESS AND LIGHT – DWELLING WHERE SCORPIONS CAN'T SURVIVE

From the example of the colors, let's look into what exists in spiritual reality. In the scripture, the concepts of darkness and light are used many times to describe the spiritual dwelling of a person. In simple terms we define darkness as where Satan abides and Light where God abides. This works to a point, but it's rudimentary. If we return to the beginning of this book, we see that scorpions are nocturnal, thus they move and hunt in the dark. In most cases during the daytime, scorpions are hiding under some rock and staying out of the light. Yet in spiritual reality, especially as we are pursuing our prophetic intercessory prayer group or walking in the office of the prophet, darkness and Light are not equal opposing forces; though you would think so from our current spiritual warfare theology. From a biblical perspective, darkness is the absence of Light, and in all cases the inability to perceive a facet of Light. In other words, darkness is not a "being" that militantly confronts the forces of Light. Darkness is the result of something or someone that obscures the Light. For example, the Cherubim on the veil of the

Holy of Holies obscure the Arc of the Presence, the Divine Light. On the other hand, in the highest realm of the heavenlies, where we abide in reality with the Father, darkness does not exist at all.

> *"Indeed, the darkness shall not hide from You, but the night shines as the day; the darkness and the light are both alike to You."*
> *(Psalms 139:12/NKJV)*

The issues of darkness and Light in the spiritual worlds have more to do with spiritual quality and perception, rather than good and evil, though many times they appear as one in the same. In the Complete Jewish Bible the above verse says, *"...night is as clear as day, darkness and light are the same."* As I mentioned earlier darkness is a result of the inability to perceive Light. What is meant by this is that darkness is actually a matter of God being concealed (behind the veil), rather than an issue of good and bad. One of the attributes of concealment is *free will,* and in that free will many times we choose evil, because we are ignorant of His Light. If God was not concealed, there would be no free will and all would compulsively choose the obvious. Yet, through God concealing Himself after the fall, He gave us the choice to pursue Him. As we are transformed into His likeness through intentional pursuit, we perceive reality as He sees it and transcend the veil.

> *"He made darkness His secret place; His canopy around Him was dark waters and thick clouds of the skies."* *(Psalms 18:11/NKJV)*

These scriptures, as well as others, point to darkness as being something a little different than just evil things. In short, darkness is God's nature (or form) either totally or partially concealed from the observer. The reason a Scorpion dwells in darkness is because their spiritual quality obscures the Light. As a result, they have no true concept of Divine reality. To put it another way, they may talk about the primary colors based on what they have read or heard from another, but the spiritual quality of those colors are not a living reality within them.

As mentioned earlier, we all start in the same place, not having a concept of His Light because we lack equivalency of form. Even when we are "born again" the reality of His nature, form and quality is yet to be discovered. The Good News is that, through receiving Christ, we turn our attention to the Author and Giver of Light and begin our journey of discovery. Yet, as the Apostle Paul says:

> *"Not that I have now attained [this ideal], or have already been made perfect, but I press on to lay hold of (grasp) and make my own, that for which Christ Jesus (the Messiah) has laid hold of me and made me His own. I do not consider, brethren, that I have captured and made it my own [yet]; but one thing I do [it is my one aspiration]: forgetting what lies behind and straining forward to what lies ahead, I press on toward the goal to win the [supreme and heavenly] prize to which God in Christ Jesus is calling us upward."*
>
> *(Philippians 3:12-14/AMP)*

The Scorpion can only thrive in us, and toward us through others, when we are not in the constant pursuit of Christ's quality and form. From the viewpoint of the higher worlds where Christ sits, when a Scorpion comes into our midst and attempts to obscure the revelation of God, it's actually an opportunity for the people in the group to press through and ascend to a greater revelation of Christ-likeness.

* * * * * * *

So what is this perception of reality we need to seek? What is this "form" and quality we need to embrace so we can see as Christ sees?

Because of how the prophetic gift works, we often fool ourselves into thinking we perceive as God perceives. Just because I have seen a movie about Yellowstone National Park, doesn't mean I know what it is to live there, touch the grass, and smell the aroma of nature. The prophetic is like going to a 3D movie (or if you're a Star Trek fan, going to the Holodeck); events can be exciting and sometimes frightening. Like any good movie, you feel what the characters feel. You're moved by their experiences and impacted by the outcome. It gives you the ability to vicariously live through the story. The same is true with intercession and the prophetic. This is why many times we can have a sense of how a person or group feels and what they are going through. Nevertheless this is where things can get "shady." Attending weekly movies about space travel in 3D and Dolby 5.1

surround sound, doesn't make one an astronaut. In the same way experiencing the prophetic or the realities of intercession doesn't make a person Christ-like. At the very least, one would hope that such experiences would motivate us to reach for higher ground in our inner quality. Yet there is a strong danger of putting our confidence in our gift, rather than our walk. The Scorpion invests in our emphasis on gifts. It uses gifts like a mating dance to entice, excite and distract a person or group.

The purpose of gifts and callings are to mature the Saints (Ephesians 4:11-13). God's intention in giving us such manifestations are to beckon us to a higher place in form and quality: His-likeness. However, during seasons of transition from one place of development to the next, darkness, concealment, and obscurity become an active part of the process. From God's perspective they are not powerful evil forces pushing back the Light (as if that were possible), which is the way some may see it, but a call to a higher place of revelation and likeness. When He summons us from another chamber within His Holy Temple, it can appear that we are in a darker place than in the recent past. This is actually normal, but to some it may appear like a demonic attack, and in some cases demons may be involved. But they are not the real issue. For the person who is not in true pursuit of Christ-likeness, it's war! For a person in pursuit of Christ-likeness, opposition becomes part of the process. From God's perspective, the hindrance is the necessary resistance to build the desire for a greater transformation. You see, Satan is not an issue to God. At the Cross, evil has been completely rendered ineffective (Colossians 2:13-15). Now to the believer in pursuit of Christ-likeness, Satan is forever unwittingly part of the process of transformation.

When we first enter each plateau, its illumination or revelation is really bright. But as we continue to transform, "where we are" seems to shade or darken. This is a preparation for that next phase. It is no different than the changing of a day. When the new day appears, there is first a season of darkness (night), then the sun rises, light appears, and the day comes (Genesis 1:8; 2 Peter 1:19). Thus, with the birth of every new level and every new transformation, there is dusk before dawn.

So how does our spiritual quality and perception of reality transform? Being a member of a church is important. Reading scripture regularly, having a prayer life, tithing, and so on, can all help. But those things are only tools to address the key aspect that defines a person's spiritual quality and resulting perception of reality. Practicing these things doesn't show us our true spiritual self. In some cases, depending upon our ability to egoistically deceive ourselves, we may "feel good" that we are doing such things and when we don't do such, we "feel bad." In spiritual reality, by living in the "feels good and bad" we have actually revealed our true self. It becomes about what I do, not why I do. Thus, we mask our true condition by believing in the "feel goods and bads." When we do that, we actually hinder the process, lying to ourselves and obscuring reality.

The way our spiritual form is defined, revealed, and also changed, is by the most foundational of all spiritual substances; and it's not intellect, nor gift, nor anything in between. Our spiritual *form* begins its determination and transformation by **intention** (1 Samuel 16:7). Our intention is the key. Is it egoistic or benevolent? Is it self-centered or giving-centered (thus, Christ-centered)? If my intention in an area is egoistic, then God is concealed from me and I dwell in darkness. Then to me, God has made His canopy around Himself thick and dark (Psalms 18:11). It is in that state of darkness that many evil things can happen. If my intention is benevolent, loving, and selfless, thus Christ-like, the darkness starts to dissipate and the Light of God (that was always present, yet concealed) is revealed. As my inner quality changes I begin to perceive differently. The difference between darkness and Light is the difference between concealed or revealed, not bad or good. The difference between religiosity and *living in Divine reality* is either "doing the right things" egoistically in the dark, or "manifesting the Life things" selflessly from the Light. To the undeveloped, outwardly in the physical realm, they may look identical.

Through my *intention* comes the transformation of my inner state, quality and form. When my inner state is transformed into a similar quality as Christ, the Head of the Church, then I can see what the Head sees. The issue is, what form is He and what does He see?

"Do not lie to one another, since you have put off the old man with his deeds, and have put on the new man who is renewed in knowledge according to the image of Him who created him, where there is neither Greek nor Jew, circumcised nor uncircumcised, barbarian, Scythian, slave nor free, but Christ is all and in all." (Colossians 3:9-11/NKJV)

One of the basic fundamental truths in Christ is, if you have put on the "new man" according to His image, there is no separation, "... ***Christ is all and in all.***"Notice that the scripture states after a person is renewed according to His image, "... Christ is all..." This is difficult for us to perceive, especially when we truly haven't attained a measure of His likeness. To the fallen or carnal man, our base perception tells us we are all separate, we are all individuals. As we develop from plateau to plateau (or as Paul says, "from glory to glory") our concept of individuality is swallowed up by true reality.

When we receive Christ, as Savior, we begin the journey of spiritual development. This pursuit "should" transform us into His image (His form), and as a result, help us see reality as it truly is. To carnal men, God is concealed and they live in darkness. One of the fundamental aspects of living in darkness is that *you are an individual,* **you are alone.** If you were in a room full of people where no sound, smell, taste or touch could be experienced, and the lights were completely out (no light whatsoever), your senses would tell you that you were alone. Welcome to Sheol! On the contrary, when you receive Christ, and allow Him to transform you into His likeness, your perception will begin to change. The difference would be when *the Light* would arise in the room, you would not see individuals, you would see a large vessel (the room) reflecting aspects of the Light. You would realize that in the Light, Christ is all and in all.

This is very hard to describe in the physical world, because the physical world relates to our carnal, lost perception. Nevertheless, another possible way to describe this is with air (oxygen). Air is to us as water is to a fish. It exists all around us, it's touching us at all times, and we need it to survive. If you put us back in that room (even with the lights on), we may insist that we are each individuals and have our rights. But as soon as the oxygen is removed through the vents in the room, we cease to be individuals. We all die together. It doesn't matter who screams the loudest, who would be willing to kill for air, or who tries to outlive anyone else; we still all die together. In that moment, what gifts we had, and what personality traits our egos told us made us special, mean nothing. In that moment, we are not individuals; we are one. Actually, the reality that we all breathe the same thing tells us we're a lot more connected than we think. For that matter, in an enclosed room we actually breathe one another's air (this is true regarding the entire ecosystem of the planet). That "air" in the worlds of the spirit *is Christ,* the Breath of God. To God, He doesn't see individuals, but aspects of His Breath. each having a distinction, but no separation. All are breathing Him in and breathing Him out. What we exhale is the source of what others inhale. To God, we all breath His Breath as one.

To press the point a little further, the same is true with the cells of the body. They are all connected and the blood feeds, cleanses and unites them. The blood is the binding element and force, just like the Breath and the Light. The Blood is Christ and Christ is all and in all. If you were to isolate a heart cell and ask it about its "individual rights," tell it that it should not be a conformist and should stand out from all the rest, it would have difficulty conceiving of such insanity! That heart cell would not be capable of considering its "privilege" of being connected to the group (its heart). From its perspective, there is no other reality. To try to conceive of separation means death to the cell and hemorrhaging to the group. Such an idea just does not compute.

Because we all experience the same Blood, Breath, and Light, they are now all the same uniting force. We receive the Light, and by doing so we are One.

"This is the message which we have heard from Him and declare to you, that God is light and in Him is no darkness at all. If we say that we have fellowship with Him, and walk in darkness, we lie and do not practice the truth. But if we walk in the light as He is in the light, we have fellowship with one another, and the blood of Jesus Christ His Son cleanses us from all sin." (1 John 1:5-7/NKJV)

Notice that this scripture tells us, *"God is Light,"* there is no darkness at all. This expounds on the scripture in Psalms that said, *"The night shines as the day; darkness and light are the same."* In the above scripture there is a walking in darkness and there is a walking in the Light. The difference between the two is how we connect, and how we see ourselves and others. The key aspect of perception is how I see Oneness with and in God. The more my **intention** is transformed in similarity to Christ, my perception of separation changes; I see all as One. It does not mean that I see a bunch of people all together in the same room who are really happy about being together. I actually see only One, *"...Christ is all and in all..."* A powerful part of this scripture is the conclusion, *"...and the blood of Jesus Christ His Son cleanses us from all sin."* Many of us have been told that to approach God, we FIRST need to be cleansed by the Blood so we can be connected to Him, which is a truth. But here the reverse is stated. First we must walk in the Light AS HE WALKS in the Light, and THEN the Blood of Jesus Christ cleanses us from sin. Go figure! That's different! Why? Because blood cannot flow through a fragmented organism. It only flows when everything is connected.

The Blood of Christ gives me the right to be connected to Him, which is a collective of One. The Blood is Christ, Christ is the Body, and they are all One. He, the Father, the Spirit, *along with the Body,* **are One.** They are manifestations of the same. What keeps me connected to the Father is not my weekly repentance of "do wrongs," but my transformation of quality so I can perceive connection to Him, which is the Whole. Christ is ALL!

When a genuine perception of this reality lives in the prophetic or the prayer group, Scorpions are nowhere to be found. If they get close, they stand out like a dark spot on a light background. When our intention is born out of our pursuit of Christ-likeness, then our form changes and we begin to see the fullness of reality as it really is. There is no such thing as me being one with God first and then somewhere down the road me being one with my brother. A person who perceives *Divine reality,* even in the dimmest Light, recognizes there is no difference.

This revelation of being One is progressive. The more my intention expresses Christ-likeness, the more I take on His form. The more I resemble His form, the more I perceive the total reality as He sees it. The more I perceive the true and total reality, the more I see there is no "me" but "we," and we are all "He!" One!

> *"I in them, and You in Me; that they may be made perfect in one..." (John 17:23/NKJV)*

In the world of intercession and the prophetic (not to mention the fivefold ministry), this is essential. If this is not *the driving intention,* shaping inner form and perception, what the prophetic will breed are "fans" and not *Fullness.* Many ministries today have congregations made up of fans and not congregations who walk in the Fullness of Reality. Scorpions cannot live very long where the Fullness of God is being developed. But Scorpions love places that have "fans." Why? Because every ego wants fans and every ego knows that fans are won by performance. On the other hand, if we are truly in pursuit of who God is, then we must see the One, not just three in one, but the many in One.

"Hear, O Israel: The Lord our God, the Lord is One!" (Deuteronomy 6:4/NKJV)

"And the Lord shall be King over all the earth. In that day it shall be — The Lord is One, and His name One."
(Zechariah 14:9/NKJV)

"...that they all may be One, as You, Father, are in Me, and I in You; that they also may be One in Us..." (John 17:21/NKJV)

Other books by John Mastrogiovanni, D.Min.:

IN SEARCH FOR THE HOLY GRAIL...
"WHY MINISTERS FALL"
...the quest for restoration on behalf of leaders and congregations in a post modern world

"This book highlights the problem of failure in church leadership and **apportions responsibility for this not only on the individual, but also upon the culture of church community.** It offers grace-based, practical wisdom to help change the status quo and minimize leadership meltdown. **This is a book of hope** which provokes change. It is not just a critical review of the topic, but diagnoses solutions to the current crisis."

Geoff Newton, Pastor
All Nations Church, England

"The insightful content of this book will cause a whole body of believers and presbytery to **make a paradigm shift.** Thus empowering them to move toward a more productive and realistic approach in restoring our fallen Christian leaders."

Saundra O'Neal, Pastor/Prophet
Fountain of Love Christian Center

THE DIVINE WOMB:
The Prophetic Purpose of Women in the New Millennium

"The Divine Womb is refreshing, intelligent, thought-provoking, and a significant contribution to our understanding of women in ministry. It compels us to reexamine our preconceptions about women and God's plan for His Church."

Gerry Wilson, Senior Pastor
Kay Wilson, Associate Pastor
Arcadia Friends Community Church

"Dr. John has powerful prophetic insights regarding the Church in this hour. *The Divine Womb* is thought-provoking and challenging. I believe **it will promote a great deal of discussion that will help the Body of Christ begin to understand God's design for women** and facilitate right relationship between men and women. It is a powerful timely word."

Carolyn Suty, U.S. Director
Aglow International, San Jose, California

BEYOND REVIVAL:
Living in the Spirit of Revolution

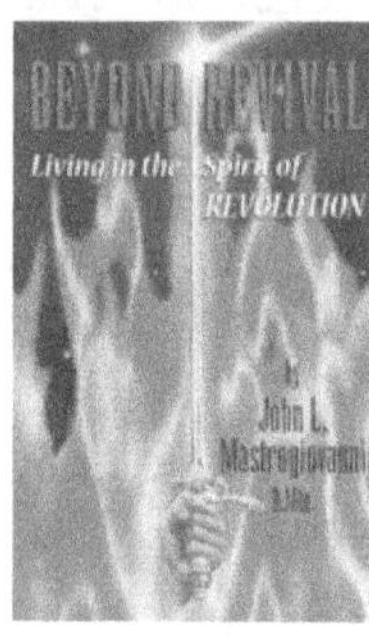

"Dr. John Mastrogiovanni offers in this book, the challenge and hope which faces every Christian disciple. **The challenge of listening to God *beyond our preconceptions* and the hope of *renewal beyond the moment.*** This book crosses all lines of theology and church identification calling for a reality of relationship with God that sparks the flame of divine movement in human history."

Rev. Gregory W. Douglass
United Methodist Church

"(Essence = the most basic, significant, and indispensable quality, property, or aspect of a thing.) Dr. Mastrogiovanni has set forth essence in Beyond Revival. **Personally, it answered many of the questions, which I have had for many years, questions that found complete resolution as I read page upon page of this God-inspired work of the Holy Spirit.** If your aim, as a church leader, is to know and follow the heart of God in church growth, ***this is a must read!***"

Dr. Earl D. Johnson
According to Pattern

You can order books or reach
John and Karen Mastrogiovanni at:

Foundation Rock Ministries or
Jesus Is Lord Christian Center
P.O. Box 1522
Monrovia, CA 91017
626-357-6797
www.jilcc.com